CAREERS

IN CHILD CARE

VGM Professional Careers Series

CAREERS
IN CHILD CARE

MARJORIE EBERTS
MARGARET GISLER

SECOND EDITION

VGM Career Books
NTC/Contemporary Publishing Group

Library of Congress Cataloging-in-Publication Data

Eberts, Marjorie.
    Careers in child care / Marjorie Eberts and Margaret Gisler.—2nd ed.
       p.   cm. — (VGM professional careers series)
    ISBN 0-658-00457-3 — ISBN 0-658-00461-1 (pbk.)
    1. Child care workers—Vocational guidance.   I. Gisler, Margaret.
II. Title.   III. Series.
HQ778.5.E24 2000
362.7'12'02373—dc21   00-44213
                                                  CIP

Published by VGM Career Books
A division of NTC/Contemporary Publishing Group, Inc.
4255 West Touhy Avenue, Lincolnwood (Chicago), Illinois 60712-1975 U.S.A.
Copyright © 2001, 1994 by NTC/Contemporary Publishing Group, Inc.
All rights reserved. No part of this book may be reproduced, stored in a retrieval
system, or transmitted in any form or by any means, electronic, mechanical,
photocopying, recording, or otherwise, without the prior written permission of
NTC/Contemporary Publishing Group, Inc.
Printed in the United States of America
International Standard Book Number: 0-658-00457-3 (hardcover)
                                    0-658-00461-1 (paperback)
01 02 03 04 05 06 HP 18 17 16 15 14 13 12 11 10 9 8 7 6 5 4 3 2 1

DEDICATION

To Shari, Anthony, and Larry—the new members of our families.

CONTENTS

ABOUT THE AUTHORS

Marjorie Eberts is a professional author who writes in the areas of careers and education. She holds an M.A. in education from Stanford University and an education specialist degree from Butler University. Her expertise in child care has evolved from 10 years of experience as a teacher along with work as a supervisor of a university reading center for children.

Margaret Gisler is a professional author and an expert in the field of child care. She has taught preschool, kindergarten, and first grade. In addition, she has been a college instructor of reading and a supervisor of a reading clinic for children. For more than six years, Margaret worked with children as a camp counselor, lifeguard, fitness instructor, and waterfront director. Her educational background includes an M.A. in education and an education specialist degree from Butler University.

Together, the two authors have written more than 70 books, usually in the field of careers and education. They have published several books for children, including a series of books on phonics and a book that teaches nutrition and shapes to preschoolers. The two authors have also written books that help parents prepare young children for school and help students learn study skills. In addition, they write a nationally syndicated column, "Dear Teacher," which gives advice to parents on how they can help their children succeed in school, and answer parents' questions on-line at www.familyeducation.com.

As the mothers of six children between them, the authors have gained first-hand experience with many professionals in the child care arena. Through their children they have been involved with teachers, tutors, coaches, camp counselors, pediatricians, pediatric dentists and nurses, private music teachers, counselors, speech therapists, children's librarians, youth ministers, baby-sitters, and child care center owners and workers as well as home-based child care providers.

CAREERS

IN CHILD CARE

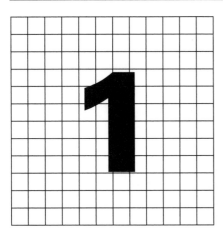

TWENTY-FIRST-CENTURY CAREERS WORKING WITH CHILDREN

Today's children are tomorrow's leaders, teachers, doctors, judges, salespeople, astronauts, and computer programmers. A child who is in school today will be president of the United States in the future. Several will be Nobel prize winners. A few will make new discoveries that will impact the lives of everyone, as the automobile and computer did in the twentieth century. The future happiness, health, and welfare of all children depend greatly upon the help they receive from all those who have careers involving their care. This book deals with those careers.

In the twenty-first century, parents will remain their children's main caregivers. They will, however, receive more help than ever before in raising their children. Parents will be directly assisted in caring for their children by child care workers in their own homes, child care centers, and preschools. Teachers from kindergarten through college will help children obtain the formal education essential to surviving in today's world. To keep their children healthy or to help them recover from illnesses or injuries, parents will rely on the professionals who have chosen careers in the health care of children. When their children have serious social or emotional problems, parents will obtain help for them from psychologists, psychiatrists, counselors, and social workers.

Parents in this new century are looking to professionals not only for help in caring, educating, and keeping their children healthy. They are also involving those who have careers that will lead to the enrichment of their children's lives. Today's parents especially want their children to acquire sports and recreational skills such as soccer, karate, swimming, gymnastics, basketball, and horseback-riding from professionals. They are also seeking to expand their children's creative skills by giving them lessons in the arts and sciences. After school and in the summer, parents are looking for youth organizations that can provide their children with such activities as camping, crafts, and scouting. Parents also expect professionals to entertain their children in movies and videos and on television, and at birthday parties, restaurants, and amusement parks.

Because parents are seeking so much help in the raising of their children, more careers than ever before are associated with children. In addition, there are careers associated with the creation, manufacture, and sale of products used primarily by children.

CAREER OPTIONS

A career that involves working with children gives many people immense satisfaction. These careers are important because the welfare of children is vital to the success of our democratic society. This book will explore a number of careers involving the care and well-being of children.

Child Care Center Careers

Fifty-five percent of all children between the ages of 3 and 5 are enrolled in child care centers, making the employment picture for workers at these centers extremely rosy. In fact, it is projected that the employment of preschool workers will grow much faster than the average for all occupations through 2006, according to the *Occupational Outlook Handbook*, compiled by the U.S. Department of Labor. Most of the 80,000 centers are nonprofit and are run by school districts, community agencies, religious institutions, and other local organizations. Businesses are also starting to operate child care facilities for their employees. Although some for-profit child care centers belong to regional and national chains, most are owned by individuals and families. The major downside to a career working in child care centers is that the pay is generally low and few benefits are offered.

Child Care Careers in Your Home

More than one million people operate in-home child care businesses, giving themselves an opportunity to work with children without leaving their homes. They have established profitable businesses that are less complicated to operate than many other businesses. Of course, it is not possible to set up an in-home child care center without complying with certain governmental regulations, and it is also essential to develop a business plan. In addition, owning a child care business involves such tasks as obtaining insurance, buying supplies, advertising services, and hiring employees. Furthermore, it is essential to be knowledgeable about child development, as a program must be created that will help each child develop socially, emotionally, physically, and mentally.

Nanny Career Opportunities

Mary Poppins is probably the world's most famous nanny. While nannies are not expected to fly through the air as Mary did, they have many of the same duties that she had. They are almost totally responsible for the care of their charges. Nannies plan the days for the children in a family and supervise most of their activities. Nannies typically live with the family, work long hours, and have weekends and holidays off. The demand for nannies is far greater than the supply. The job does require training, and most professional nannies have attended nanny school or have a background in early childhood education.

Baby-Sitting Career Opportunities

Baby-sitting is a less formal job than being a nanny. Baby-sitters usually go to a home to help working parents or parents who want a night out or a short vacation together. Baby-sitters may also baby-sit children in their own homes. Baby-sitting is often an intermittent or part-time job. A baby-sitter typically watches the children of just one family. However, two or more families may get together to hire a sitter. Wages are generally paid on an hourly basis. There is a tremendous demand for baby-sitters, especially those who have proved reliable.

Education Careers Working with Children

The teaching profession is the largest in the world. From Aristotle to this year's teacher of the year, the task of teachers has always been to help other people learn. Teaching as a profession has developed largely since the 1800s, when teacher-training schools opened in western Europe. Teachers in preschool and Head Start (see Chapter 2) programs are usually required to have taken several courses in early childhood education. Kindergarten, elementary, middle school, and junior high teachers, however, normally have bachelor's degrees. A career in teaching is an investment in the next generation.

Children's Sports and Recreation Careers

Many of today's children are filling their leisure time with organized sports and recreation activities. They are eager for sports instructors to teach them sports skills or how to become more adept at a sport. Their interests in sports range widely from the traditional, such as tennis, swimming, and basketball, to the less well known, such as archery, karate, and canoeing. Children also seek recreation through some form of play, amusement, and relaxation. Recreation workers help children learn how to use their leisure time effectively. They work at recreation and parks departments, at summer camps, and with civic, social, fraternal, or religious organizations.

Children's Health Careers

Health care professionals have the opportunity to exercise the compassion they feel for children in a meaningful way. They diagnose illnesses, perform medical examinations, and treat children suffering from injury, disease, and mental health problems. At the same time, they advise parents on their children's diet and hygiene and on preventive health measures. Most careers involving the health care of children require special training and licensing. Certain health care careers, such as pediatric cardiologist and child psychiatrist, demand years of postgraduate training and education. Employment of health care professionals is expanding rapidly as more emphasis is placed on preventive medicine and as new technologies emerge.

Careers Ensuring the Welfare of Children

Children can be the victims of poverty, family problems, and abuse. Some children join gangs, commit crimes, and do not attend school regularly. Choosing a career in child welfare or juvenile justice is an opportunity to make the world a better place for children who find themselves in unfortunate situations and to rehabilitate those who exhibit antisocial behavior. Such careers require individuals who are mature, objective, and extremely sensitive to children and their problems. Social workers, police officers, juvenile court judges, court referees, and child advocates are concerned with ensuring children's welfare. They find jobs in child welfare departments, police juvenile bureaus, adoption agencies, crisis intervention services, schools, hospitals, clinics, and social service organizations.

Arts and Entertainment Careers with Children

Artists, dancers, and musicians share their expertise with children as they teach them these arts. Just as many children are attracted to sports, many are also drawn to learning how to play musical instruments, dance, and draw pictures. Children gain pleasure from acquiring skills in the different arts, and they also enjoy being entertained. Clowns and magicians amuse children, and so do actors in children's theaters and on radio and television programs designed for children. Careers in entertaining children are for those who want to bring enjoyment to children while satisfying their own desire to be in front of a camera, microphone, or audience.

More Careers Working with Children

Jobs helping and caring for children are found just about anywhere there are children. At a library, children's librarians help children select books. Artists may concentrate their careers on capturing images of children on canvas or in stone. Children's book illustrators bring authors' tales to life. Salespeople in children's shoe stores fit children in the correct shoes, and clerks at toy stores help children choose toys. In churches, youth ministers tend to the spiritual needs of young people. An amazing variety of jobs exists for those who want careers working with children.

ASSESSING CAREER APTITUDES

Are you interested in a career that will let you work with children? The following questions can help you assess which career areas relating to the care and well-being of children are most appealing to you.

1. Am I primarily interested in teaching children?

2. Is the health care aspect of caring for children my major interest?

3. Do I want to work directly with children, or would I rather work in a job dealing with their care or well-being?

4. Do I prefer to work with a specific age group, such as newborns, toddlers, preschoolers, or school-age children?

5. Do I prefer working with both children and their families?

6. Would I rather work with one child, a few children, or a group of children?

7. Do I want to work in an office, child care center, home, clinic, or hospital?

8. Do I want to establish my own business?

9. Would I like to supervise other employees?

10. Do I want to work in the private or public sector?

11. Do I want to work for a profit or nonprofit business or organization?

12. Would I prefer to work for a small, medium, or large business?

13. Am I willing to get training or a college degree in order to pursue my career interest?

14. Am I willing to read constantly to keep abreast of what is happening in my career field?

15. Do I truly like children so much that I want to devote my career to their care and well-being?

LOOKING AT THE FUTURE

Children are not spending as much time with their parents as they once did. In the twenty-first century, this time will decrease further as more mothers join the workforce. Parents will rely even more than they do today on other caregivers to nurture, teach, and guide their children. This trend will result in more jobs in almost every area dealing with the care of children. In fact, it is anticipated that employment of workers in child care will increase much faster than the average for all occupations through 2006.

Today, the majority of people in careers associated with the care and well-being of children are women, and it appears that this will not change in the immediate future. In addition, many of the jobs relating directly to the hands-on care of children are poorly paid. Advocacy groups are capturing the attention of the media with their campaigns describing child care workers as underpaid and undervalued. The goal of this work is not only better pay for child care workers, but also greater recognition from the public for their efforts.

FINDING OUT MORE ABOUT CAREERS IN CHILD CARE

An excellent source of information for most careers related to child care is the *Occupational Outlook Handbook*, compiled by the U.S. Department of Labor. Consult this book before making vital career decisions. The book gives information about working conditions, employment opportunities, training required, advancement opportunities, earnings, and future job outlook for most types of work. It can be found in libraries, bookstores, and on-line at http://stats .bls.gov/blshome.htm.

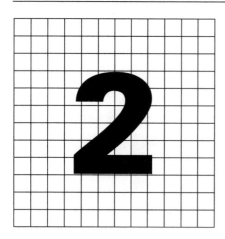

CHILD CARE CENTER CAREERS

The U.S. labor force has experienced a revolution with the entry of working mothers in dramatic numbers. As recently as 1975, only one-third of women with children worked outside the home. Now, approximately 70 percent of all mothers work. This group includes everyone from the computer programmer working 10-hour days to the part-time worker teaching four hours a week. The major impact of this change in the workforce is the overwhelming demand that now exists for child care workers. And this demand is increasing each year as the number of working mothers continues to rise.

THE DEMAND FOR CHILD CARE WORKERS

The number of married mothers joining the workforce increased rapidly during the 1980s both for mothers of children under 6 and for those of children between 6 and 17. For example, in 1980, 45.1 percent of all married women with children under 6 were employed outside the home, but by 1990, that had shifted to 58.9 percent. And for women whose children were over 6, participation in the workforce rose from 61.7 percent in 1980 to 73.6 percent in the 1990s and the numbers continue to rise.

Separated, divorced, and single mothers of young children have always worked outside the home in greater numbers than married mothers. While their participation in the labor force increased during the 1980s, the increase was not as dramatic as it was with married mothers. In the 1990s, approximately 60 percent of separated mothers and 70 percent of divorced mothers with children under 6 were working mothers. The percentages increased greatly for those whose children were over 6. About 75 percent of separated mothers and 86 percent of divorced mothers with older children were in the workforce. As more and more mothers join the workforce, more child care workers are needed.

The increased number of working mothers is the number-one reason why demand for child care workers has skyrocketed. Furthermore, as their children move through school, there will be a need for more child care workers for supervision of before- and after-school activities and during vacations and holidays from school.

The other reason is the very high turnover rate among child care workers. According to *The National Child Care Staffing Study, 1988–1997,* the average turnover of all staff at child care centers in 1997 was 31 percent. More than 27 percent of assistants and 39 percent of teachers left their jobs. The explanation for this turnover is quite simple: it's the money, or rather the lack of it. The wages for child care workers, including the highest-paid staff members, are abysmally low. The same study also indicated that in 1997 the highest-paid child care teachers at centers earned barely half as much as nearly 74 percent of professional workers.

CAREER OPTIONS FOR CHILD CARE WORKERS

As the number of working mothers has increased, a need for a variety of child care arrangements has emerged. This, of course, has created many career choices that center on the care of children. Although approximately 20 percent of all families rely on relatives for satisfactory child care arrangements, the rest must look for help beyond their immediate family circle. The two most popular choices are child care centers and family child care homes. This chapter explores the different types of child care centers and the job opportunities they offer. Careers in family child care homes will be investigated in Chapter 3.

HISTORY OF CHILD CARE CENTERS

Before the Industrial Revolution, children were typically cared for in their homes by their families or by caregivers hired to assist family members. In the mid-1700s, factories sprouted up all over England and Scotland, and large numbers of women left their homes to work in them. This change was due largely to the invention of two machines, the spinning jenny and the water frame, which took the manufacture of textiles out of homes and into factories. Women were not able to leave their young children at home nor have the children at their sides in the factories while they were working. To solve this problem, factory owners established rooms for their workers' children and hired untrained adults, boys, and girls to supervise the children. These were the first child care centers. The establishment of child care centers in the United States occurred almost 100 years later, when manufacturing became a major industry and women first joined the workforce.

Besides pioneering child care centers, Great Britain also introduced nursery schools a short time later to improve upon the care children were receiving at factory child care facilities. Robert Owen, a mill owner and social reformer, set up the first program to teach and supervise the children of factory workers and hired people with some teaching qualifications

During World War II, women were needed to work in the factories. The U.S. government responded by passing the Lanham Act, which provided funds to set up child care centers in defense plants. At the end of the war, these centers were shut down, and many women left the workforce. In the 1960s, 1970s, and 1980s, women began returning to the workforce and the need for child care centers grew. Today, more than 80,000 centers serve 55 percent of children ages 3 to 5.

In the mid-1960s, the federal government began to play a more prominent role in the care and development of young children. The Head Start program was launched to help prepare the children of poor families for school. Activities were designed to stimulate the social, emotional, mental, and physical growth of young children. Many parents of children in this program work in centers as aides or as volunteers. The Head Start program continues today. Also, the federal government began to provide some child care services for mothers receiving welfare payments who were enrolled in job training programs.

Many proposals for federally sponsored child care programs have been introduced since the 1960s. A comprehensive proposal, the Child Development Act, was passed in Congress in 1971 but was vetoed by President Nixon. This legislation would have expanded Head Start and provided preschool education for all children who needed this help before enrolling in school. Every year child care bills are introduced in Congress; however, no comprehensive national child care plan has yet emerged. Some states have begun to offer prekindergarten programs for 4-year-olds in their most disadvantaged school districts. And others are considering legislation requiring all schools to offer programs for 3- and 4-year-olds. A wide variety of child care programs are subsidized by federal, state, and local governments, and more will appear in the future to meet the demand for quality child care. At all levels of government, regulations have been issued that set standards for providing quality child care. One of the most common regulations is the establishment of ratios for how many children of a certain age can be cared for by one child care worker.

During the 1980s, business and industry became aware that working mothers with young children had more absences from work and left their jobs more often due to the responsibility of caring for their children. The problems were greatest with the mothers of preschool children. In response, employers devised child care options to help their working mothers. A few have developed both on-site and off-site child care centers. In some cases, a group of employers have joined together to provide child care for their employees. An employer may also establish a referral service to help families find child care. Many employers offer vouchers for child care or include some form of child care in their benefits packages. With research showing that employer-sponsored day care programs improve morale and cut personnel costs, more companies have started some type of child care program. This trend is expected to continue, and to accelerate, in the future.

TYPES OF CHILD CARE CENTERS

While all child care centers are organized to care for young children, there is diversity in the ownership of these centers. Most centers are operated by nonprofit organizations. Although people hear a lot about national child care chains, most of the for-profit child care centers are locally owned. The ownership composition of child care centers is shown in Figure 2.1.

There are advantages in having so many different types of child care centers. Not only do parents have a choice, but child care workers also can choose the work environment that is most appealing to them.

Nonprofit Child Care Centers

Two-thirds of all child care centers are nonprofit centers. They are operated by religious organizations, YMCA groups, public schools, parent associations, local organizations, recreation and park districts, and government services. These centers vary immensely in their size and the services offered. A center may have just one room with a teacher and an assistant teacher or several rooms and more than 20 staff members. It may be licensed for 20 children or more than 100. Nevertheless, nonprofit child care centers generate the greatest number of positions for child care workers.

Step One School, in Berkeley, California, is an excellent example of a nonprofit child care center. The center is a nonprofit public benefit corporation governed by a board of directors. The staff consists of codirectors and 19 teachers, of whom 60 percent work a part-time schedule of five to six hours. The teachers are salaried and are also paid overtime for meetings and conferences. The school has an innovative benefits program that lets staff apply benefits dollars to the specific benefit programs they want. This saves both the center and the employees money.

The school is easily accessible by public transportation. The building, formerly a K–3 public school, is situated on a prime site with views of San Francisco Bay. It contains five sunny and airy classrooms and a kitchen. The fenced yard provides a safe area for climbing, sand play, bike riding, and just sitting on the grass. A shrub-covered hill has trails for hiking and exploration and space for gardening.

Figure 2.1 Ownership of Child Care Centers

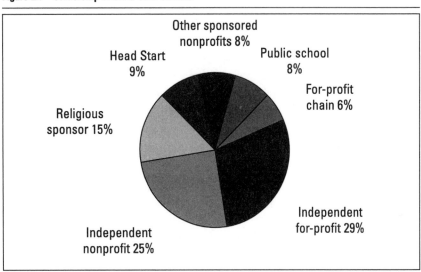

Source: A profile of child care settings

The goal at Step One is to guide the development of a well-rounded child— one who knows and trusts himself or herself, who can get along with others, and who can recognize and follow his or her interests as well as create new ones. Both the indoor and outdoor environments are carefully designed by the staff to set the stage for play, which is the work of the child.

The children learn through experimenting, playing independently, building, and engaging in games and art projects they find attractive and interesting. Through their play and social interactions, the children discover more about the world they live in, build concepts, and learn to express their feelings in appropriate ways.

The school offers four programs: a program for 2-year-olds, a nursery school program, a kindergarten program, and an afternoon program that extends care for children in the morning program. The teachers for each of the programs work together to develop an overall schedule of activities that meets the needs of the children. The curriculum is planned each week at classroom team meetings in which the events and progress of the last week are evaluated and new projects are developed collectively.

Step One has an open admissions policy that accepts children on a first-come, first-served basis, with adjustments for age and sex. The school is committed to having a diverse population of families and actively recruits in the community to achieve this. Step One also has an active scholarship program.

For-Profit Child Care Centers

Approximately 35 percent of all child care centers are for-profit. Most are independent rather than being part of a local or national chain. Teachers and assistant teachers usually receive hourly wages. The general rule regarding benefits is the smaller the center, the fewer the benefits.

Kid Time, in Walnut Creek, California, is a good example of a small, for-profit child care center. The school is principally owned by Stephen Wilson, who teaches at the center and who founded it along with his father. As is typical of small centers, the director also teaches. All together, four full-time teachers and an assistant teacher care for approximately 35 to 40 children each day. As the enrollment climbs during the year, more staff is hired to keep the teacher/child ratio within state requirements. The director of Kid Time is salaried, while the teachers receive hourly wages. Some medical benefits are available for the staff. The center provides five sick/personal days, one week of vacation after one year of employment, and paid holidays.

The school is open all year except for eight major holidays. Hours are from 7:00 A.M. to 6:30 P.M., which are standard operating hours for many child care centers. Classes are offered for toddlers, preschoolers, and prekindergartners. More than half of the children stay all day. The morning program is basically preschool in nature, and some preschool work is also done in the afternoon.

Kid Time is located in an old home that has been expanded to accommodate the center. The atmosphere is intentionally very homelike to help the young children make a smooth transition between home and center. There is a large room for classes, another room for conducting group activities, and a kitchen, bathroom, and utility/art room.

For-Profit Child Care Chains

Only 6 percent of all child care centers are operated by chains. Nationally, there are two giants: KinderCare, with over 1,000 centers, and La Petite Academy, with more than 730 academies. These chains have standardized curriculums, policies, and operating rules. They offer considerably more amenities and services than the smaller child care centers, but their tuition is usually higher. For child care workers, employment with national chains usually means the opportunity to have some benefits, such as medical, dental, and life insurance, and 401(k). Smaller neighborhood centers typically will not be able to offer these benefits.

In recent years, the chains have been expanding into new areas by opening centers in places close to parents' workplaces. In addition, centers that cater to children ages 6 and up have been started. They offer only before- and after-school care, including taking children to school and picking them up after.

Employer-Sponsored Child Care Centers

Although employers are definitely concerned with the issue of child care, few companies actually offer it on-site. One of the best-known facilities is the Hacienda Child Development Center, located in its own building in the Hacienda Business Park in Pleasanton, California. The center has received international recognition for its innovative design, which features large windows and spacious outdoor play areas. Such amenities as a partially covered outdoor play area, air-conditioning, and radiant heating provide for the children's comfort and necessities, even in extreme weather.

The Hacienda Child Development Center offers the services that most working parents require. It is open from 7:00 A.M. to 6:00 P.M. five days a week and operates year-round on a business calendar. Employees working in the Hacienda Business Park receive a discount, as do employers who become corporate associates or corporate members of the Early Learning Institute (ELI), which operates the center. ELI operates its own centers as well as private centers under management contracts.

The professional staff receive a salary based upon their education and experience. Permanent, full-time staff receive health, dental, and vision insurance, retirement plans, flexible pretax spending accounts, child care subsidies, a credit union, paid holidays, seniority sabbaticals, sick and vacation days, and paid time off for program observations, jury duty, and bereavement. In all programs, the center exceeds the minimum staffing ratios required by state law. The infant program maintains a maximum 3 to 1 ratio rather than the required 4 to 1 ratio, while the toddler program maintains a maximum 4 to 1 ratio. The 2-year-old and preschool programs maintain maximum 8 to 1 and 10 to 1 ratios, respectively, rather than the state 12 to 1 requirement.

The center offers care for infants, toddlers, preschoolers, kindergartners, and first and second graders. The infant and toddler programs are based on ELI's innovative HeadsUp! approach, which makes use of play and learning games to help lay the necessary foundations of all future learning. The preschool program is a modified Montessori curriculum incorporating art, music, and imaginative play into the traditional emphasis on practical life, sensorial, language, mathematics, science, and cultural activities. The elementary program comprises a self-paced, individualized curriculum that continues and expands upon the Montessori curriculum employed in the preschool program.

The center makes a strong effort to keep parents involved. Parents receive written daily activity reports. They are also urged to attend the parent education meetings held once a month to keep parents informed on a wide variety of topics.

Extended-Day Child Care Centers for School-Age Children

The most rapidly developing area of child care is extended-day child care. This care is offered at hours when school is traditionally not in session and is designed for children who are enrolled in kindergarten through junior high or middle school. These programs are operated by a wide variety of institutions including schools, child care centers, home-based child care providers, recreation centers, and youth-serving organizations. Many programs offer van service to and from the schools the children are attending or are located within walking distance of the schools. Extended-day programs typically offer homework time, supervised care, and indoor and outdoor space for play. Some programs also offer enrichment, academic instruction, and special classes in areas such as dance, computers, music, and various sports.

The demand for more extended-day child care programs increases the need for child care workers. At child care centers that also care for younger children, existing personnel as well as part-time workers will provide the care. At centers that offer only before- and after-school care, personnel will work just during these sessions.

APTITUDES OF A CHILD CARE CENTER WORKER

The number-one requirement for individuals considering a career working in child care centers is a sincere desire to work with children. To be an effective worker, a knowledge of child development and child-rearing practices is also a prerequisite. In addition, certain aptitudes are key to working well with children. Child care workers need to have:

- Nurturing skills

- Sensitivity to the feelings of children

- Excellent communication skills with children

- An abundance of patience

- A calm disposition

- A tolerance of the clutter that surrounds young children

In doing this type of work, it is also essential to have good health, since child care workers are exposed to many illnesses while working with young children. Furthermore, it is helpful to have the physical stamina to bend and lift both children and materials throughout the day. Because children are so energetic, child care workers need to have a lot of energy. Skills in music, art, drama, and story-telling are important, too.

Child care workers work closely with other employees at a center. For example, three or four teachers and assistant teachers may be caring for thirty 3-year-olds within one room. In this situation, considerable cooperation is required to handle the children. For this reason, child care workers need to be willing to be team players who listen to each other's suggestions and readily share ideas.

TRAINING

In the past, it was possible to work at a child care center with no qualifications except an ability to work well with children, or even just an interest in working with children. While it still may be possible in a few states to find a job at a center with absolutely no training in early childhood education or development, most states now have legislation requiring child care workers to have taken certain courses or training in order to be hired. California is one state that demands that child care workers have considerable course work in early childhood education in order to work in private and public child care centers. The following employment requirements state the training applicants must have in order to work in private and public child care centers in California. Note that more training is required for public centers than private centers.

Private Centers in California

Aide. Aides must be at least 18 years of age, be high school graduates, and be under the supervision of a qualified teacher at all times.

Teacher. The state requires teachers in private centers, both profit and nonprofit, to complete a minimum of 12 units at the college level of early childhood education courses with at least one course in each of the following areas:

- Child development/psychology (3 units)

- Child, family, and community (3 units)

- Curriculum (6 units)

Some private centers may hire as teachers individuals who have completed 6 units of early childhood education courses, provided they are currently enrolled in a further 6 units.

Director. Directors must have the 12 units of early childhood education required for teachers, 3 units in administration, and four years of experience in a licensed center. Individuals with an associate of arts (A.A.) in early childhood education need two years of experience in a licensed center plus 3 units in administration, and those with a bachelor of arts (B.A.) in early childhood education need a children's center supervisory permit or one year of experience in a licensed center in administration.

Additional classes in safety and health, such as CPR and first aid, may be needed to work at a center. Also, the requirements to work at a center for school-age children are slightly different.

A Child Development Permit is required to work in state-funded early child care and development programs. The six levels of permits include the education and experience requirements in Table 2.1.

Child Development Associate Credential

Many states require child care workers to have the Child Development Associate (CDA) credential offered by the Council for Early Childhood Professional Recognition. The CDA program consists of two parts: CDA training and CDA assessment. The training portion, which teaches skills needed by child care center workers and home-based child care providers, is offered in local schools and colleges. Completion of the training program is not required for assessment, but assessment is necessary to obtain the credential. The assessment is made by a team of child care professionals from the Council for Early Childhood Professional Recognition. It involves showing the team that the applicant has the required skills and knowledge about child care, whether acquired through formal training or experience. You can obtain more information about eligibility requirements and a description of the credential by contacting Early Childhood Professional Recognition, 2460 16th Street NW, Washington, DC 20009.

Table 2.1   Education and Experience Requirements for Child Development Permits

Title	Education Requirement	Experience Requirement
Assistant	6 Units of Early Childhood Education (ECE) or Child Development (CD)	None
Associate Teacher	12 units ECE/CD including core courses	50 days of 3+ hours per day within 2 years
Teacher	24 units ECE/CD including core courses + 16 GE units	175 days of 3+ hours per day within 4 years
Master Teacher	24 units ECE/CD including core courses + 16 GE units; + 6 specialization units; + 2 adult supervision units	350 days of 3+ hours per day within 4 years
Site Supervisor	A.A. (or 60 units) with 24 ECE/CD units (incl. core); + 6 units administration; + 2 units adult supervision	350 days of 3+ hours per day within 4 years, including at least 100 days of supervising adults
Program Director	B.A. (or 126 units) with 24 ECE/CD units (incl. core); + 6 units administration; + 2 units adult supervision	Site supervisor status and one program year of site supervisor experience

Source: State of California

Associate of Arts and Bachelor's Degrees in Early Childhood Education

The associate of arts (A.A.) in early childhood education is typically a 60-semester-unit program at a community college. Individuals have to fulfill general degree requirements by taking classes in such subjects as English, mathematics, science, and history, plus classes in early childhood education. The advantage of an A.A. is that these classes can usually be transferred to a college or university and used toward getting a bachelor's degree. And of course, each additional degree applicants have only makes them more attractive as candidates for jobs in the child care field, as well as helps them start their careers further up on the career ladder.

Only a few child care centers require applicants to have a bachelor's degree in order to qualify for teaching positions. However, this degree does give its holders a chance to start at many centers as a head or lead teacher. It also is a prerequisite for many positions as assistant director or director.

POSITIONS FOR CHILD CARE WORKERS

The job titles used to describe child care workers vary from center to center. There is no standardization. The number and type of positions found in any center largely depend on its size. At a large child care center, the career ladder would look like this:

director
assistant director
head teacher
lead teacher
teacher
assistant teacher

The duties of both assistant teachers and teachers at a center depend greatly on the age level of the students. Teachers of infants and toddlers must necessarily spend considerable time in supplying basic care to the children. Diapers must be changed, bottles must be given, noses must be blown, shoes must be tied, children must be held and hugged, and assistance must be provided at mealtimes. The younger the children are, the greater the amount of attention that must be directed to caring for them. At the same time, it is important for the teachers to create an atmosphere in which the children can have a variety of experiences so that they will develop socially, emotionally, physically, and mentally. As the children grow older, teachers are able to concentrate more on giving the children educational experiences and less on supplying basic care. When the children are school-age and in extended-day child care programs, their teachers supervise their care, help them with homework, and plan recreational activities.

The Personal Story of an Assistant Teacher

The entry-level position at child care centers is assistant teacher. The title of *aide* is frequently used to describe the job, as is *teacher assistant*. This is the one position in child care centers that does not require any early childhood education courses in some states. The main duty of the assistant teacher is to help the teacher in the classroom so that the program runs smoothly. In many centers, however, the assistant teacher and the teacher or teachers with whom he or she works share the tasks equally or almost equally.

Jane Kocourek is an assistant teacher of 1-year-olds at one of the child care centers of a national chain. She is beginning at this level because she has not had the early childhood education courses required to be a teacher in California, even though she has been a kindergarten teacher in another state. Jane and the other teacher share equally in the responsibilities of caring for eight young children. At all times a ratio of four children to one teacher must be maintained in keeping with state regulations on the number of children a teacher of 1-year-olds may supervise. Each teacher does what is necessary at a given moment for the children in his or her room, following the general guidelines spelled out by the national chain for this age level. A typical schedule for Jane's day looks something like this:

8:00 A.M. On arrival, Jane usually sits on the floor playing with and talking to the children. She may even read stories to them. Diapers are changed as needed in the morning.

9:00 A.M. Snacks are served at a table. One teacher will clear the snack while the other remains with the young children. After the snack, the children go outside and play in the yard. Both teachers supervise this outside play session.

10:30 A.M. Lunch is served. The cook brings the meal to the room. While one teacher serves, the other sits with the children who require a little assistance to eat their lunch. After lunch, the children again play outside for approximately 20 minutes while both teachers watch them play.

11:30 A.M. The children lie down for their naps after all have had their diapers changed. The room is darkened, and the teachers use the first few minutes of naptime to wash the children's personal cups and bottles, remove garbage, and return luncheon dishes to the kitchen. When these tasks are completed, Jane goes to another area of the center and pulls out over 60 cots for the older children.

12:00 P.M. Jane enjoys a one-hour lunch break. As an hourly worker, she is not paid for this time.

1:00 P.M. Jane spends the next hour doing special tasks for the assistant director and director. One day she may trace letters for a bulletin board while on another she may supervise a group that is napping.

2:00 P.M. The 1-year-olds start waking up. Jane returns to the room and reads stories to some of the children as the others begin to wake up. She may also lead them in movement exercises to music. Then it is time to change all the children's diapers and serve the afternoon snack before going back outside again with the children.

3:30 P.M. The children return to their room and play with the blocks, manipulatives, and riding and pushing toys. Some may dress up, and others may play with the toy kitchen. Jane and the other teacher supervise their play and may suggest activities.

5:00 P.M. Parents begin to arrive to take the children home. Jane has to stay until the number of remaining children is four or fewer. Her workday officially ends at 5:00 p.m. so she receives overtime pay for additional time spent at the center.

Jane feels that she provides important nurturing to the children and helps them in learning verbalization skills. The children are getting a highly qualified assistant teacher who truly cares about them. When Jane obtains her California teaching credential, she plans to leave the child care center and to find a job teaching kindergarten.

The Personal Story of a Teacher

Alice Bush works at a child care center that was designed for the parents who work in the business park where the center is located. She is an experienced teacher with a bachelor's degree in child development and has worked in Montessori child care centers. Alice has had considerable training in the Montessori approach, which is based on the philosophy of Maria Montessori, an Italian physician and educator who made remarkable progress with the education of slum children in Rome in the early part of the twentieth century. The cornerstone of the Montessori approach is a respect for the child as an individual striving for independence. The role of the Montessori teacher is to observe each child carefully and to facilitate learning through the child's own experiences. Alice utilizes her special training at the center, which follows a modified Montessori approach.

Alice works from 11:00 A.M. to 6:00 P.M. teaching 30 children between the ages of almost 3 through 6. A head teacher, a lead teacher, and another teacher share the teaching responsibilities with her. The head teacher makes up the daily schedule, which is the same every day. The following describes Alice's day at work:

11:00 A.M. When Alice arrives, the children are outside in their play area. All of the teachers are supervising the children, making sure they are safe. None of the teachers are assigned to a specific group of children. Most of the time the children are engaged in free choice of activities; however, Alice or one of the other teachers may set up a game or a project, possibly doing something in the vegetable garden.

11:30 A.M. The children return inside for a group reading session. While one teacher reads to the children, the others are busy directing hand washing and bathroom activities, setting up for naptime, and organizing lunch. The teachers take turns handling these activities.

12:00 P.M. The children eat the lunches they have brought from home.

12:30 P.M. The older children leave to take part in the kindergarten program, which is held in another room. The rest of the children go down for naps. Alice stays with the nappers. While the children are resting, she is busy writing the daily reports that tell parents what their children have done that day. She also makes the afternoon snack and develops materials that will be used with the children.

3:00 P.M. The kindergarten children rejoin the group, and all enjoy a snack outside. Activities are low-key and similar to the earlier period outside. The head teacher goes in to do preparation work.

4:00 P.M. When the children return inside, the group becomes smaller as parents pick up their children. One of the teachers leaves. Alice may do preparation work or tell the children a story.

4:30 P.M. Alice will work with the children on an art project, direct a movement activity, or have the children play a musical game.

5:00 P.M. At 5:00 P.M. and 5:30 P.M., the other teachers leave, depending on the number of remaining children. Alice is then alone with the children, supervising them as they play with manipulatives, blocks, and other classroom materials. At the same time, she is checking the identification of parents and talking to them about their concerns.

Alice is committed to working with children. She fully believes the Montessori approach is the way to educate children for life. She plans to take more Montessori training to get her Montessori certificate.

What Being a Head Teacher Is Like

Within most child care centers, several teachers and assistant teachers work together in a classroom supervising the children and presenting educational activities. The teacher who is ultimately responsible for coordinating the efforts of all the teachers, taking care of the administrative work, and consulting with parents is called either a *lead teacher* or a *head teacher*, depending on the center. At some centers there is a head teacher as well as a lead teacher. In this case, the head teacher has the ultimate responsibility for the program, does the administrative work, and talks with the parents, while the lead teacher oversees what is happening in the classroom.

What Being an Assistant Director Is Like

The role of assistant director is not well defined. Quite often assistant directors are also part-time teachers. At some centers they will only handle administrative paperwork, while at others they may be in charge of the curriculum. Many child care centers, even large ones, do not have assistant directors. The one responsibility all assistant directors share is stepping in for the director whenever he or she is not at the center.

Suzanne Cox is the assistant director at one of the centers of a very large national chain of child care centers. Her only child care jobs have been at this center, where she started as a part-time assistant teacher with just three units of early childhood education. Suzanne swiftly advanced to teacher, as soon as she had sufficient early childhood education units, and then to assistant director, all within one year of starting at the center. She describes the position of assistant director as that of a director in training. Her duties and responsibilities at the center include:

- Handling the center's banking and bookkeeping

- Organizing all of the children's files

- Keeping track of immunization records

- Contacting substitute teachers

- Stepping in as a substitute teacher

- Administering medicine to children on medication

- Preparing accident reports

- Contacting parents of sick children

- Documenting and conducting fire drills

- Handling special projects such as writing a new curriculum for foreign students attending the center

- Driving a van run

Suzanne's duties are typical of assistant directors at centers associated with child care chains. She works from 8:00 A.M. to 5:00 P.M. She receives an hourly wage plus a benefits package that includes free child care for her daughter. Suzanne likes working for a national chain because it is easy to transfer to another center.

The Personal Story of a Director

The director has the ultimate responsibility for all facets of the operation of a child care center. Depending on the ownership, he or she will justify the operation of a center to a board of directors (nonprofit), a divisional manager (chain), or an owner or group of owners (independent, for-profit). By studying the day of a director, it is possible to understand how many tasks directors must handle.

Being a director, according to Linda Owens, is akin to being an expert in crisis management, since the director is responsible for every aspect of running a child care center. This can mean coming to the school at 1:00 A.M. when the burglar alarm goes off or finding yourself driving the early run of the center van because the van driver called in sick at the last minute. In addition, the director is the one who has 100 percent responsibility for the profit and loss of the center.

Linda is director of a child care center with a capacity of 160 children. Currently the enrollment is 130 children, and the center has 22 teachers and assistant teachers (aides). Because she works at a child care center that is part of a national chain, she is responsible for following the company's policies and daily procedures.

As director, Linda has an amazing number of duties and responsibilities, including the following:

- Following all state regulations for child care centers

- Making sure the chain's curriculum is being followed

- Handling parental and staff complaints

- Hiring and firing center staff

- Making sure that tuition is paid for all children

- Counseling children with behavior problems

- Marketing the center

- Conducting monthly staff meetings

- Acting as a substitute teacher when necessary

- Visiting with parents as children are left off and picked up

- Providing tours of the center to prospective clients

- Making sure that the kindergarten is following state guidelines

- Checking that field trips are properly staffed

- Ensuring that the building is maintained in a proper manner and is clean

Linda holds an A.A. in early childhood education and is currently working on her master's in human development and counseling. Before becoming a director at this center, Linda was a teacher, an assistant director, and a director at another center. She plans to continue in her present work because she enjoys helping families care for their young children.

LOOKING AT CHILD CARE CENTER WORKERS

By sex. Overwhelmingly, child care center workers are female, including the administrative positions of assistant director and director. Furthermore, positions in upper management, such as regional and divisional directors of national chains, are predominantly filled by women.

By age. According to *The National Child Care Staffing Study,* the teaching staff of child care centers is young. The majority are 40 years old or younger. Half of the teaching staff is under 30, but only 21 percent of the directors are. Also, the study found that 41 percent of the teaching staff had children and that 46 percent of the entire staff had children who were younger than school age. Many staff members brought their children to work with them and received either a tuition reduction or free child care, depending on the center.

By education. The majority of the staff at child care centers, even assistant teachers, have had some formal course work in early childhood education or child development. As to be expected, the higher workers rose on the child care center career ladder, the higher their level of education was. *The National Child Care Staffing Study* found that 44 percent of the teaching staff had some college and 22 percent had bachelor's degrees or more. The study also found that 25 percent of the staff had professional certification in such areas as elementary or secondary education, nursing, social work, and miscellaneous fields.

The Personal Story of a Founder of a Child Care Center

Sue Britson had a dream of founding a child care center that would reflect her philosophy. She firmly believed that children's development—socially, emotionally, mentally, and physically—began at a very young age and wanted to influence their development and work with their ideas. Sue had a master's degree in early childhood education plus several years of teaching experience. This gave her a solid background in understanding how child care centers operate, which is something needed to successfully establish a center.

The first step in starting up a school, according to Sue, is to decide upon your philosophy and mission. Then, by researching what other centers exist in an area, you can determine the appropriate niche for a new center to fill.

Next, you must find a suitable location for the center. A center for young children should be located in a safe area that is easily accessible to families, preferably near public transportation. In addition, Sue points out that the location must be zoned or capable of being zoned for a child care center. In selecting a site, be sure to consider whether the building meets, or can easily be made to meet, local and state licensing regulations. Passing an inspection from the local fire marshal is part of the process of selecting the right building for a center. And, of course, you will need seed money to start up: at least two months of operating expenses in the bank would be a sufficient amount.

Sue and her partner found a site in June in a room in a community recreation area. In September, their center opened, and classes were full within a week. From the first day, their center was a success because parents were so pleased to find professional teachers (with education and training) operating a center that stressed a developmental approach. Within two years, the partners and codirectors of the center realized that they must expand in order to pay themselves a living wage. Besides teaching at the center, Sue had to work 30 hours a week as a waitress to survive.

After carefully doing their research again, they relocated in a former K–3 school that was sold at an auction. This site offered five classrooms, a fenced yard, and an office complex. When the center reopened, it had an expanded high-quality program taught by professionals, and the teaching staff began to receive benefits and better wages. (The school is described earlier in this chapter.)

SALARY AND FRINGE BENEFITS

Child care workers are underpaid. *The National Child Care Staffing Study, 1988–1997* found that the wages of teaching staff were at subsistence levels. The 1997 study showed that since the original study in 1988, there were modest increases in real wages only for the highest-paid teachers and the lowest-paid assistants. Although child care workers have higher levels of formal education than the average American worker, their wages are substantially lower.

Figure 2.2 shows that real wages for child care workers remained stagnant in the 90s. Figure 2.3 shows the low wages child care teaching staff typically receive, and Figure 2.4 shows the wages child care workers are receiving in comparison with the average wages for nonmilitary workers with various education levels. According to the 1997 Office of Current Employment of the Bureau of Labor Statistics, only 14 occupations report having lower median wages than child care workers.

Child care workers are constantly exposed to illness at work, which poses a serious risk to their health. Their health benefits are improving, especially for teachers, but according to *The National Child Care Staffing Study, 1988–1997*, only 21 percent of centers offered fully paid health coverage to teachers and assistants. And of those centers, fewer than 23 percent provided health coverage to dependents.

GETTING HIGHER WAGES FOR CHILD CARE WORKERS

The low wages of child care workers are beginning to get the attention of the general public because of the actions of advocacy groups. One effort promoting action by child care workers and care providers to secure a living wage and decent working conditions for themselves is the Worthy Wage Campaign. The first national Worthy Wage Day was April 9, 1992. This day was designed to call attention to the low pay that child care workers receive and also to teach child care workers that it is perfectly acceptable for them to speak up about their low wages. On this day, workers were urged to take time off from their jobs to march, rally, and wear buttons to make the public aware of their need for "worthy" wages. Since then, many community leaders have joined the Worthy Wage Campaign to urge livable wages for child care workers.

Figure 2.2   Trends in Hourly Wages for Center-Based Child Care Staff

Staff Position	1986 Wages	1992 Wages	1997 Wages	Real Change Between 1992 and 1997	Real Change Between 1986 and 1997
Lowest-Paid Assistant	$5.99	$5.91	$6.00	1.5% increase	0.17% increase, or $0.01 per hour
Highest-Paid Assistant	$6.96	$7.03	$7.00	0.43% decrease	0.57% increase, or $0.04 per hour
Lowest-Paid Teacher	$7.38	$7.55	$7.50	0.86% decrease	1.6% increase, or $0.12 per hour
Highest-Paid Teacher	$9.53	$10.33	$10.85	5% increase	13.9% increase, or $1.32 per hour

Source: Reprinted with permission from the Center for the Child Care Workforce. Copyright © 1999 by the Center for the Child Care Workforce, 733 15th Street NW, Washington, DC 20005; 800-U-R-WORTHY; ccw@ccw.org.

Figure 2.3   Average Annual Earnings of Child Care Teaching Staff, 1997

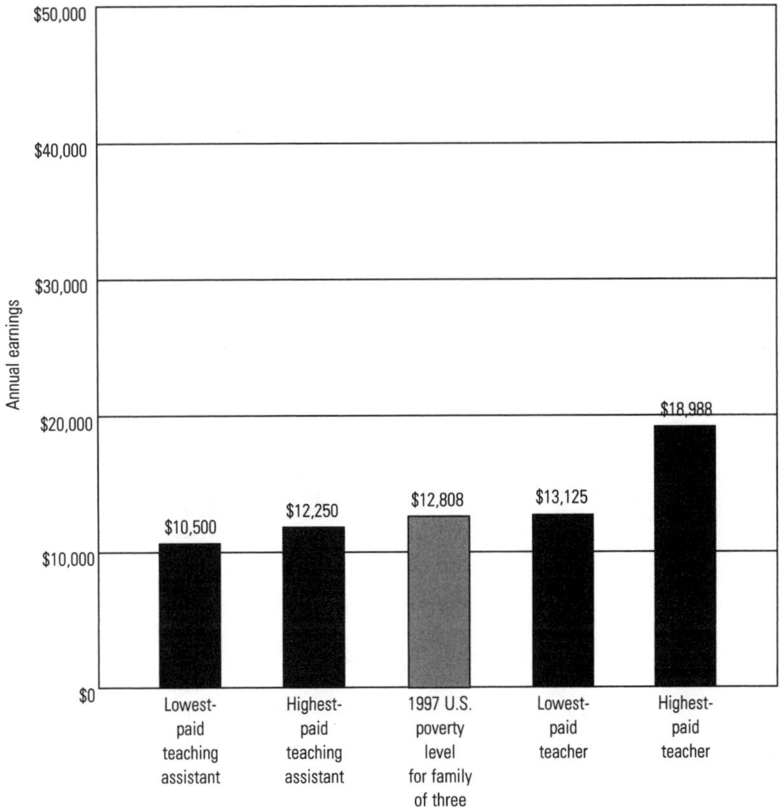

Note: Full-time annual earnings based on 35 hours per week/30 weeks per year—the average workweek of teaching staff in the original sample.

Source for poverty level figure: U.S. Census Bureau.

Source: Reprinted with permission from the Center for the Child Care Workforce. Copyright © 1999 by the Center for the Child Care Workforce, 733 15th Street NW, Washington, DC 20005; 800-U-R-WORTHY; ccw@ccw.org.

The Personal Story of a Worthy Wage Program Associate

Kate Ashby worked as a Worthy Wage Program Associate at the Oakland-based Child Care Employee Project, which had taken on the mission of getting higher wages for child care workers. Kate truly knew what it meant to be underpaid for working in child care. After graduation from college, she worked in another field, but teaching children was always her true career goal. So she went back to school and obtained a master of education in early childhood education. Her first job in early childhood education was at an outstanding school closely associated with a university. While the school was a wonderful place to work, this highly educated teacher's wages were only $10 an hour, which did not give her even $1,000 a month in take-home pay. Her low wages were made up for in part by her benefits, which were very generous. After a year, however, Kate moved and started working at a new school. Her wages increased to $13 an hour, but she had no benefits

Figure 2.4 Child Care Workforce Earnings in Perspective

A comparison of median hourly wages between child care jobs and other occupations

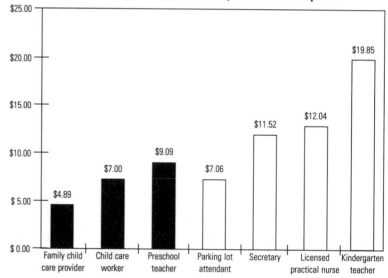

Source: Based on Bureau of Labor Statistics Data 1997; compiled by the Center for the Child Care Workforce. Reprinted with permission from the Center for the Child Care Workforce. Copyright© 1999 by the Center for the Child Care Workforce, 733 15th Street NW, Washington, DC 20005; 800-U-R-WORTHY; ccw@ccw.org.

and was not working full time. Kate's effort to stay in the early childhood field is representative of the struggle most child care workers face.

THE FUTURE

The nurturing, caring people who work in child care centers gain great satisfaction from working with children. They are, however, dissatisfied with their salaries and benefits. Steps are being taken to address this problem. State spending on preschool is growing, and low-income families are receiving vouchers for child care in many states. States are beginning to offer scholarships to child care providers to pursue more training. The federal government is forgiving college loans for those who study and work in the field of early childhood education, as well as providing the states with Child Care and Development Block Grant money to improve salaries and benefits.

The future as a worker in a child care center is much brighter than in the past. First of all, the demand is high and will remain high for teaching staff. In addition, some centers are already paying their staff a satisfactory wage. Finally, the attention being focused on low wages makes it more likely that child care workers' salaries in the future will reflect their vital contributions to families and the nation.

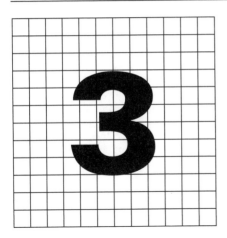

CHILD CARE CAREERS IN YOUR HOME

The child care delivery system has become a big business in the United States. New solutions to the problem working parents face in finding quality services for their children are emerging. Working parents can now choose from a wide variety of caregivers. The type of caregiver families use seems to differ according to the children's ages. When the families of employed mothers seek care for children younger than age 3, they choose almost equally between child care centers, family child care homes, and relative care. Child care centers are discussed in depth in Chapter 2. Family child care homes offer the care of a single caregiver who may or may not have a helper. Children are able to establish a firm bond with the caregiver, which is more difficult to achieve at child care centers, where the staff turnover rate is high. In addition, the children are in a homelike atmosphere with fewer children than in a child care center.

APTITUDES OF A FAMILY CHILD CARE PROVIDER

Over one million people have chosen careers as family child care providers. Most are women. They are not just people who happen to care for children in their homes but are professionals who offer a valuable service. To be successful, it is essential to be more than just a nurturing individual who loves children. The daily care of several children is challenging. Emergency situations must be handled. A solid developmental program for the children needs to be created and followed. The children must be shown how to play together. Parents who consistently pick their children up late or fail to pay on time must be dealt with. A family child care provider should possess the aptitudes described in Chapter 1 plus these special ones:

- Ability to take responsibility for the total care of several children

- Ability to juggle several activities at one time

- Willingness to work long hours

- Toleration of the wear and tear on the caregiver's home

- Willingness to commit to caring for children in the caregiver's home for a year or more

- Ability to discipline in a positive manner

- Willingness to create a program that meets the individual needs of each child

- Willingness to share information about each child's progress with parents

- Capability of offering the children a safe environment

- Ability to select and keep competent help

- Ability to deal effectively with parental complaints

- Good bookkeeping skills

- Willingness to keep accurate records for each child

- Ability to handle business aspects of child care professionally

ASSISTANCE FROM CHILD CARE RESOURCE AND REFERRAL AGENCIES

A child care business can, of course, be started without too much preparation. However, to be a professional in this area, more is required. A license should be obtained, information and business forms for parents should be created, one or more rooms in the home should be set aside and prepared for the children, and a program of activities for the children must be developed. Fortunately, agencies throughout the country offer services to prospective family child care providers. These child care resource and referral (CCR&R) agencies give child care providers the training, technical assistance, and support to develop high-quality child care programs. At the same time, they also help parents make informed choices in selecting care.

The number of CCR&R agencies has grown steadily since the 1980s, matching the increasing need for child care. Most CCR&Rs are private, local organizations created by parents or child care advocates. Only a few CCR&Rs are state or public agencies. Funding is provided by a combination of monies from city, county, state, and federal governmental units, businesses, corporate foundations, United Way agencies, service organizations, charitable organizations, and individuals. Approximately half of the states possess statewide networks that offer training and technical assistance to local CCR&R agencies. Before deciding to start a family child care home, prospective care providers should always consult with their local CCR&R agency. Information on the location of the nearest CCR&R agency can be obtained by contacting the National Association of Child Care Resource & Referral Agencies, 1319 F Street NW, Suite 810, Washington, DC 20004, visiting their website at www.naccrra.org, or by calling the Child Care Aware number, 800-424-2246.

The Personal Story of a CCR&R Agency Employee

Phyllis Graser was one of the thousands of CCR&R employees who offered services to parents and child care providers. She worked for a private, not-for-profit corporation that had three area offices and two satellite offices. The offices offer the following services:

Parent services

• Referrals

• Subsidized child care

• Parent education

Provider services

• Provider development

• Nutrition education

• Recruitment/training

Advocacy

• Seminars and conferences

• Speakers bureau

• Bimonthly newsletter

Employer services

• Feasibility study

• Needs surveys

• Tuition assistance management

Agencies as well as offices of an agency do vary in the breadth of services they offer. At her office, Phyllis was the only employee. Besides helping parents find quality child care, she provided assistance to family child care home providers in these areas:

Licensing. Phyllis held orientation meetings to introduce prospective caregivers to the licensing process, which in her state is lengthy. Individuals need step-by-step guidance to complete this process.

Start-up meeting. Phyllis conducted a monthly orientation meeting on the business aspects of starting a home child care business. Help was given with marketing, insurance, taxes, and record keeping.

Referral list. Phyllis called local child care providers once a month to update the agency's list of licensed child care providers. Also, she checked on the number of spaces available by age level at the family child care homes.

Provider development. Phyllis arranged classes in cardiopulmonary resuscitation (CPR) and advanced training workshops for home caregivers. She also worked with individual providers to help them offer quality child care.

Child care food program. Child care providers are reimbursed by the Department of Agriculture for a portion of the cost for nutritious meals served. Phyllis linked providers with nutrition and health experts within the agency who assisted with meal planning and the paperwork necessary to become part of the food program.

PREREQUISITES FOR SETTING UP A FAMILY CHILD CARE HOME

Many steps are involved in setting up a quality family child care home. First of all, it is necessary to decide whether your facility will be independent or associated with an organization. Many organizations, including churches, charities, and businesses as well as state and local government units, will contract with individuals to care for children in their homes. Not only will they help caregivers set up a home facility, they will also provide the children and pay for each child. The organizations typically provide advice on operating a family child care home and may offer some benefits. The disadvantage to this arrangement is that the caregiver largely becomes an employee rather than the owner of an independent business.

Checking on Governmental Regulations

Family child care providers will need to get a license to operate their businesses in most cities. They should also find out if any other city agencies have jurisdiction in setting up a family child care home. In addition, zoning regulations should be investigated. It may be necessary to go through the permit process. This involves proving that there is sufficient on-site parking for the employer and any employees, enough play area for each child, no concentration of child care facilities in the neighborhood, and an adequate pickup area for parents. It is best to check out all possible regulations before establishing a family child care business.

Obtaining a License

Prospective caregivers must determine whether a state license is required to operate a family child care home. Some states have very stringent requirements, and others have practically no requirements at all. The nearest CCR&R agency can provide this information, as can the state department responsible for licensing homes for child care. Licensing requires caregivers to meet certain minimum standards for health, safety, and staffing. For example, family child care homes in California must meet the following standards:

- Fingerprint and tuberculosis clearance of all adults over age 18 in the home

- Certain fire and safety standards for the house

- Prohibition of all physical and humiliating punishment

- The right of parents to visit the home at any time

- Guns and ammunition locked up

- No smoking while children on premises

- **Small-home license:** Eight children, provided two of the children are of school age, or only four children if under age 2.

- **Large-home license:** Fourteen children with no more than four under age 2, and an aide present for seven or more children.

Family child care providers do not need to be licensed in California if care is provided to the children of only one family. Parents, however, can require providers to get a physical examination and TB clearance, present references, take CPR and first aid classes, and offer a smoke-free environment.

Getting a license when one is not required can seem unnecessarily time-consuming. On the other hand, parents tend to prefer family child care homes that are licensed because it implies professionalism and means that minimum standards have been met.

Becoming an Accredited Caregiver

Caregivers who want to be recognized as professionals providing high-quality care seek accreditation from the National Association for Family Child Care (NAFCC). Accreditation scrutinizes the following content areas: relationships, environment, activities, developmental learning goals, safety and health, and professional and business practices. The process involves using a self-study workbook to assess the caregiver's own program, designing a professional development plan to prepare for an observation visit, and making quality programs. In order to be eligible for NAFCC accreditation, a caregiver must meet these requirements:

- Offer care to children in a home

- Be the primary caregiver (children are not left with a substitute more than 20 percent of the time)

- Be at least 21 years old

- Have a high school diploma or GED

- Have 18 months of experience as a family child care provider (at the time of the observation visit)

- Have 65 hours of documented training (completed before the observation visit)

Participating in the Child Care Food Program

Family child care providers should investigate the Child Care Food Program (CCFP). The program, which is sponsored by the U.S. Department of Agriculture (USDA), reimburses child care providers for a portion of the cost for meals served. Its purpose is to improve the diets of children by offering well-balanced, nutritious meals and to help providers serve high-quality meals without passing the cost on to working parents. The program is administered locally through sponsors. CCR&R agencies sponsor the food program in many areas or know the name of the area sponsor. Furthermore, many sponsors will help with the program's paperwork, have menu suggestions, and provide nutrition education. Each month the home caregiver has to complete forms showing the number of meals and snacks served and menu forms. The meals must meet USDA requirements. It is necessary to reapply for admission to the program annually.

ORGANIZING THE BUSINESS SIDE OF A FAMILY CHILD CARE HOME

Getting insurance, filing and paying taxes, keeping good records, setting fees, and writing contracts will play an important role in the operation of a quality child care home. Most CCR&R agencies will provide expert help in these areas. For example, some agencies have books with forms that can be used for keeping records, bookkeeping, and contracts. Moreover, through agency education programs and newsletters family child care providers can keep abreast of any changes in laws that may affect them.

Getting Insurance

One day Johnny hits Susie and stitches are required, or a parent trips and falls walking up the drive of the caregiver's home. Accidents happen, and child care providers need the protection of insurance from their first day of operation. Caregivers should be aware that homeowner's policies do not normally cover the operation of an in-home business. And unfortunately, the rates of insurance for child care providers have risen dramatically in recent years. The homeowner's insurance agent can give solid advice about insurance coverage and possibly place a rider on the existing policy to cover claims related to the child care business. Caregivers should also find out if insurance can be purchased through a local child care association.

Filing and Paying Taxes

Family child care providers need to pay federal and state taxes. It is also necessary to pay social security taxes for the caregiver and any employees. CCR&R agencies may have helpful materials or workshops devoted to the handling of taxes. In addition, the *Tax Guide for Small Business*, available from the Internal Revenue Service, is loaded with helpful information on filling out forms and on keeping books and records.

Keeping Good Records

If family child care providers don't keep good records, they will never know whether they are making a profit. Records are also needed to support all items of income and expense reported on tax returns. A bookkeeping system should be chosen before the business opens. It is helpful to have a separate bank account for business income and expenses. A petty cash fund should be established for small expenses. The invoice, paid receipt, or canceled check should be saved for every expense in a safe, well-organized file. Although most caregivers remember to keep a record of expenses for food, toys, helpers, and supplies, they may forget such items as professional magazines, organization dues, a percentage of the house utility bills, and fees for insurance premiums.

Setting Fees

To some degree, fees are determined by what other family child care providers within an area are charging. Study the marketplace to find out what other caregivers are charging and then set a fee that will cover your expenses and produce a certain income. The local CCR&R agency should have information on low, middle, and high fees within the community. Where a caregiver lives can affect the fees he or she is able to charge. Rural, small-town, and inner-city providers may be able to charge only $50 or less per child per week. On the other hand, suburban and high-income-area caregivers may be able to charge more than $150 per child per week. In setting fees, it is essential to consider the following factors:

- The basic fee and how many hours are included
- Charges for additional time
- Charges for late pickup
- Meals and snacks to be included in fees
- The rate structure for different ages
- Charges for absences
- Discounts for siblings
- Charges for supplies (diapers, crayons)
- Charges for holidays

Once fees are set, create a policy sheet listing the fees and exactly how and when they are to be paid.

Writing a Contract

Contracts eliminate misunderstandings. They should spell out the rules under which the family child care home will operate. Parents need to know if care will be available on holidays, how arrivals and departures will be handled, and whether the children can bring toys from home. The contract should also include the fee schedule. Figure 3.1 consists of a sample contract from a CCR&R agency that caregivers can adapt to meet their needs.

SETTING UP A FAMILY CHILD CARE HOME

After organizing all the business aspects of a family child care home, it is necessary to set up the home itself. Physical changes may have to be made to the caregiver's home to provide an appropriate environment for children. Space will

Figure 3.1   Sample Family Child Care Contract

CONTRACT

Date_____

I agree to enroll my child _____age_____ in the
_____Family Child Care Home, beginning on
_____. I have received and read the Family Child Care Home Rules
and agree to comply with all rules and responsibilities as stated. This contract
will be valid beginning_____. Two weeks notice by either party will be
required in order to terminate this contract. This contract will be revised on an
annual basis. Care will normally begin at _____ o'clock and end at _____ o'clock
on the following days of the week:_____.

Care will/will not include the following meals and snacks:_____.

The charge for care of the child is $_____ per_____. Overtime
charges are $_____ per_____.

Parents are expected to pay full rates for holidays, absences, and parent vacations.
Additional charges will be accrued for special dietary requests or damages to the
contractor's property.

Payment to the Family Child Care Provider will be made in advance.

Parents are to provide the names of any persons authorized to pick up children,
medical and insurance information, and any special dietary or health concerns.

(Optional) Payment obligation is based on the hours parents contract to use
child care.

_____

Provider Signature

_____   _____

Parent Signature   Address/Phone

_____   _____

Parent Signature   Address/Phone

_____

Date

Source: Contra Costa Child Care Council

be needed for eating, sleeping, and playing. Many caregivers have to remodel part of their homes to acquire sufficient space. Frequently, garages are turned into interior play space. In addition, the outside play area will need to be fenced. All areas that the children will use must be made safe. This includes locking up or storing out of the children's reach all hazardous materials, knives, medicines, and matches; covering electrical outlets with safety caps; and locking up any guns or ammunition. A cubbyhole or bin should be provided for each child to use for storing extra clothing and take-home items.

The exact tools of the trade needed to launch a family child care home depend on the ages of the children for whom care will be offered. Caregivers will probably need most of the following items:

- Cribs, cots, or sleeping mats

- Television set and videocassette recorder (VCR)

- CD player and CDs

- Books, puzzles, and games

- Blocks and balls

- Manipulative toys such as Legos, small figures, and Tinkertoys

- Assorted toys from trucks to trains

- Art and craft materials

- Child-size tables and chairs

- Dress-up clothes

- Play kitchen and/or playhouse

- Dolls and stuffed animals

- Sandbox and sandbox toys

- First aid kit

- Emergency supply of diapers and baby food

Not all of the materials will have to be purchased. Caregivers may already own many of the items. Friends may contribute toys and furniture to the caregiver, and some items can be borrowed from CCR&R agencies.

CREATING A FAMILY CHILD CARE PROGRAM

The most important aspect of establishing any family child care home business is developing a sound program for the children. Caregivers need to realize that young children learn through play. Having an adequate supply of playthings is essential so that the children can experiment, build, play games, and enjoy art activities alone and with others. The children's time should be divided between free choice of activities and group activities such as stories, music, and movement.

Every day should have the same general schedule that can be adjusted to meet the children's needs. Before a family child care home opens for business, a daily schedule of activities should have been well thought out.

Child care providers who do not have a background in early childhood education should make use of the informational programs and materials offered by CCR&R agencies and child care associations. They also should take courses in child care and child development, which are readily available at community colleges.

MARKETING THE FAMILY CHILD CARE BUSINESS

Once the home is prepared and the program is devised, the caregiver needs to market his or her service to families within the community who are looking for child care. Local CCR&R agencies can serve as advertisers. They provide parents seeking child care with the names of licensed caregivers, and they regularly update the number of current openings available by age group. To attract business, caregivers need to market their service in a variety of ways in order to gain exposure to the widest possible number of prospective clients. Some suggestions on how to market a family child care business follow.

Word-of-mouth. Tell everyone about the business; someone is certain to need child care services. It may turn out to be a friend of a friend or an acquaintance of the supermarket clerk.

Flyers. Colorful flyers that attract attention should be placed in spots where working parents are likely to see them, such as on bulletin boards at grocery stores, churches, and YMCA/YWCAs.

Newspaper ads. Placing ads in local newspapers, including shoppers, is another way to reach potential clients. Ads should specify the age groups for which care is offered, the hours of care provided, the special competencies of the caregiver, and the general location of the home.

Newsletters. Companies, organizations, and churches often publish newsletters that have advertisements or occasionally write about services family child care homes offer.

The Personal Story of a New Family Child Care Home Provider

Maureen B. Chahin has just started Kid Kelly Play and Learn, a family child care home. She is now caring for five children between the ages of 18 months and $3^{1}/_{2}$ years in her home. One of the children is her own daughter. Maureen brings to her new business a solid background in early childhood education, having taught preschool, kindergarten, and elementary school in the past. She launched this business because she wanted to be near her daughter and liked working with children. With the help of her husband, she has approached starting her new business very professionally. By looking at the steps Maureen followed, we can see the actual effort required to start a family child care home business.

Step 1. Maureen attended the orientation class for prospective family child care home providers at the nearest CCR&R agency. She also purchased the agency's book, which contained sample forms and information on how to start up a family child care home.

Step 2. The licensing process for a large-home license (12 children) was initiated. Maureen and her husband took TB tests and were fingerprinted. The backlog was so great that it took 92 days to get fingerprint clearance. The fire marshal visited three times before being satisfied that the home had met fire safety standards. More fire extinguishers and smoke detectors had to be installed. The major problem was finding a fire alarm that could be heard throughout the neighborhood.

Step 3. Maureen and her husband attended a business class at the CCR&R agency.

Step 4. Maureen obtained a business license from the city and checked to see that there were no zoning problems.

Step 5. Maureen's husband contacted their insurance agent over the phone and arranged accident and liability insurance.

Step 6. A bookkeeping system was established, as well as a file for storing receipts and pertinent business information.

Step 7. Maureen assessed the suitability of her home. The family trilevel home was perfect for caring for the children: the entire lower level could be used for the children. The family room became the children's playroom, and the bedroom was set up with cribs and cots for napping. There was also a bathroom and a door to the yard on this level. Gates had to be installed to keep the children from leaving the lower level as well as entering the upper level. One advantage of the trilevel home was that Maureen could prepare meals and snacks in the kitchen and see what the children were doing in the play area because of the openness of the house design.

Step 8. The yard was landscaped to provide a safe play area for the children. Soft bark was placed under the swing set, a sandbox was built, and a water table was installed.

Step 9. Maureen purchased sturdy toys, books, records, puzzles, a play kitchen, a push train set, and blocks to create a playroom full of exciting possibilities for the children to explore.

Step 10. Maureen decided on her policies and made up a parent handbook that covered her philosophy, the admissions policy, a statement of the rights of the licensing agency, and policies on arrival, departure, late pickup, and absence. The handbook also detailed her health and nutrition policies and how accidents and medication would be handled. Information was provided on clothing, napping and rest time, the children's cubbies, artwork, birthdays, field trips, toys from home, and discipline. A thorough explanation was given of the program, tuition payment policies, and the use of a parent's bulletin board to enhance parent/caregiver communication.

Step 11. Maureen engaged her sister as her helper and investigated the possibility of getting a high school student in the early childhood training program as a helper later on.

Step 12. Maureen began marketing her family child care home. She placed a notice in the neighborhood home-owner's newsletter and received five or six inquiries from this source. Word-of-mouth brought more prospective clients from a friend who ran a child care facility that was full. She ran an ad in the local newspaper and put flyers up at the local park and neighborhood stores. Her informative flyer is shown in Figure 3.2.

Step 13. Maureen received many phone calls about her child care business and began to show the home to interested parents. Almost everyone who saw the quality setup decided to enroll their children in her program.

Step 14. A daily schedule of activities was formulated for the children.

Step 15. The family child care home opened for business, and an information folder was created for each child.

Step 16. Steps were taken to enroll the home in the Child Care Food Program to get reimbursement for meals and snacks.

The Personal Story of an Experienced Family Child Care Home Provider

For 18 years, Norma Manning has been caring for children in her home. She has stayed with this career so long because she truly enjoys being around children. Norma wants her home to operate like a warm family group. Norma belongs to an association of caregivers that meets monthly. She finds these meetings helpful because the caregivers share ideas, and there is always a speaker on a subject that interests her. For example, she may learn more about preparing healthy snacks, dealing with difficult children, or following the latest regulations.

Norma's daily schedule is flexible. Some days she takes the children to the park or on a shopping expedition. She typically cares for six to eight children of

Figure 3.2   Flyer for a Family Child Care Home

 Kid Kelly

Play and Learn
Tender Loving Child Care
in our Shadow Creek home.
California credentialed Teacher
with 7 years preschool, day care,
elementary school experience
enjoys working with Children!!!
Lots of fun activities daily.
Big backyard with
Sandbox, Swings, Castle & Water Table
Openings Available
18 months and up

Please Call Maureen
at 555-4052 to
make an appointment
to come by !!!!!!!

diverse ages with the full-time help of a former kindergarten teacher. The daily schedule at Norma's home usually follows this pattern:

7:00 A.M.–9:00 A.M. The children arrive and are given breakfast, if needed.

9:00 A.M.–10:00 A.M. The children play alone or in groups with the variety of toys and games in the playroom. Some will watch television or Disney programs on the VCR. All the children are fascinated by Norma's two parrots. They especially like to handle the tame little parrot. Norma teaches them how to be gentle with the parrots and her other animals.

10:00 A.M.–11:00 A.M. Most days the children are able to play outside. Much of their play centers around the large two-story playhouse Norma designed and had built. They also are able to enjoy playing with Norma's two lop-eared rabbits, a very big cat, and two puppies.

11:00 A.M.–12:00 P.M. The children return inside to work on age-appropriate activities with Norma's helper. They will usually hear stories, sing songs, and do some preschool readiness activities.

12:00 P.M.–1:00 P.M. The children have their lunch after washing up from their outdoor time.

1:00 P.M.–3:00 P.M. All the children have a rest time. The younger children nap.

3:00 P.M.–5:00 P.M. The children play inside and outside under Norma's watchful eyes until they are picked up by their parents. A few children will remain after 5:00 p.m. because their parents commute or work late.

FOSTER CARE HOME PROGRAMS

While family child care home providers give home care to children when their parents are working, foster parents care for children in their homes around the clock for days, weeks, and months. The children have been placed in foster care because their own families cannot provide adequate care for them. Foster children are of all ages, from newborns to teenagers. All of the children have suffered the trauma of being separated from their parents, and many have been in several foster homes. Frequently, they have been abused or neglected by their parents. They may be malnourished or ill. Some have problems with schoolwork. Others are immature and do not relate well to their peers. Foster children require special help physically, mentally, socially, and emotionally. They need guidance and affection from mature adults in a solid home environment. Foster children especially need to develop a sense of security and healthy self-esteem. Foster care ends when a child reaches age 18.

The demand for foster parents is enormous in every area of the United States and is steadily growing even greater. The foster care system is overwhelmed by the number of children needing care. Much of the increased demand for foster care homes can be attributed to the rising level of substance abuse by parents.

What Being a Foster Parent Is Like

Not everyone is cut out to be a foster parent. The personal demands are great. A concern and affection for children is absolutely essential, as are the necessary skills, stamina, and patience to deal with children who often have serious problems. Foster parents must be able to accept the temporariness of their jobs. They play a critical role in working toward the reunification of the children with their families, or when this is impossible, in helping the children to adjust to a permanent placement. In addition, foster parents need to work well as part of a team that includes social workers, court representatives, counselors, and health care professionals.

In order to be a foster parent, it is essential to obtain a state foster care license. The state will set the number of foster children that a home can care for based on the number of beds, bedrooms, and the ages of the children. Even though licensing requirements will vary between the states, they usually include the following guidelines:

- Foster parents need to be over age 21. They can be single or married.

- Foster parents must have sufficient income to support their own families without relying on foster care payments. Both parents can work if it does not adversely affect the care of the foster child.

- Foster parents must be fingerprinted and pass a criminal background check plus a general character interview.

- Foster parents need to have good health and the stamina to deal with the problems of foster children.

- Foster parents need to provide solid references.

Help Is Available for Foster Parents

Foster parents do not face the enormous problems of helping foster children alone. Whether they work for a public or private agency, they will attend orientation meetings to acquaint them with what foster parenting is like. In-service training will prepare them to work with foster children. And there will be newsletters continually updating them on all the services available to foster parents. Once they are on the job, there are continuing workshops for foster parents plus classes at community colleges. In addition, most foster parents join local associations that meet monthly to discuss mutual problems and to hear speakers on subjects involving foster parenting skills. These groups offer an excellent opportunity to network with other foster parents. Furthermore, each child's caseworker visits the child and the home regularly and assists the foster parents in helping the child. Special help is also available from counselors, health care professionals, and the Department of Social Services.

The Rewards of Foster Parenting

Foster parents receive a monthly payment for each child that is designed to cover food, clothing, and recreation. Medical care is typically paid for by the state. If a child remains with a family for a year, the parents can receive a tax break by counting the child as a dependent. The foster parent program is not designed to offer any more financial remuneration than the cost of caring for a child or children.

The rewards of being a foster parent lie in the satisfaction of helping children who are desperately in need of a stable home life. Foster parents lend a helping hand to children when this assistance is needed. They have the gratification of making a difference, often a profound difference, in a child's life.

The Personal Story of Foster Parents

Steve Warga and his wife, Karen, are licensed to care for five children in their home. They are currently foster parents to four children. In the three years that they have been caring for foster children, they have had seven children in their home. Steve works outside the home, but his wife is a full-time caregiver of the children, who are typically newborns to 3-year-olds. All of the children for whom they have cared have had parents with substance abuse problems. Most of the children had been in several foster care homes before they came to the Wargas'. Their first foster child, who was 4 years old, had already been in four foster homes. His sister, who was $5^1/_2$, had been in five homes in two and a half years before she came to the Wargas'. The Wargas are going to adopt these children. Another child came to them as a premature infant of a substance-abusing parent. Today, that child is healthy and will soon leave their home. Another brother and sister only stayed at their home for a short time because their parents were able to turn their lives around and care successfully for their children. Unfortunately, not all foster children return to parents who can give them the needed care. One of the toddlers for whom the Wargas are now caring will probably be placed permanently in their home, since the mother has shown no concern about the child.

Steve points out several things that prospective foster parents should know. First of all, foster parents do not have to accept all children. They have the right to know about a child's background and to see a child before making a decision to have the child in their home. He also says that foster parents must work closely together to devise ways to handle these children. Many of the children who have been assigned to their care have been hyperactive, a condition that requires very skilled parenting. Finally, Steve admits that though foster parenting is challenging because the children need a high level of care, the opportunity to really help a child brings immense rewards.

ANOTHER CAREER POSSIBILITY: GROUP HOME CARE

Throughout the country, groups of children are cared for in homes and on the grounds of residential centers in cottages or in large buildings. The children in these homes may be foster children or children with serious disabilities. Child care workers are needed in all of these facilities. In many cases, the workers are expected to act in a parental role. This means they will share a family life with a small group of children. They will see that the children do routine tasks in the home, help them with their homework, and try to make the children feel comfortable, secure, and cared for. At times, a married couple may work together in a group home. There are also group homes where child care workers do not play a parental role but rather care for the children under the direction of a supervisor.

The demand for child care workers in group homes is high because the pay is usually low and the work can be very difficult in homes where the children have serious problems. Workers typically receive room and board at residential facilities and often will have paid vacations, health insurance, and other benefits.

THE REWARDS OF CARING FOR CHILDREN IN A HOME SETTING

Caring for children in one's home lets caregivers help the children of working parents develop in a home environment. At the same time, home caregivers have the pleasure of establishing a business in their own homes while contributing to the well-being of a future generation. Foster parents and group home workers have the reward of providing a helping hand to children when it is really needed. All child care workers have the satisfaction of enriching the lives of children.

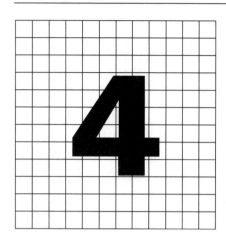

NANNY CAREER OPPORTUNITIES

The nanny profession emerged in England, where the original nannies were trained at the Norland Nursery Training School. On the job, they wore starched black uniforms with white aprons, little black hats, and sensible, sturdy shoes. Today's nannies receive their formal training in community and nanny colleges and dress casually for work in jeans and sneakers. While Mary Poppins, the well-known fictional nanny, flew through the air with the Banks children, nannies are now found skateboarding with their charges. Many are also college graduates earning as much as other young professionals.

DEMAND FOR NANNIES IS HIGH

Nanny placement agencies in hot markets like New York, Los Angeles, and Boston never have enough nannies to meet the demand.

Read the following advertisements from the classified section of a major metropolitan newspaper in the Midwest and note the range of positions open for the employment of nannies:

Nannies—Immediate placement for part-time, full-time, temporary nannies. Please contact Indy Nannies Plus, (317) 555-7711.

Nannies—Needed for East Coast placement. Positions available immediately. References required. Call Nanny Hotline (212) 555-Nanny.

NANNY—Loving, exp'd, responsible. M–F. NE side 3 young children. 555-9872.

Nanny—Part time. Needed for daughters ages 12 and 14. Evenings and weekends. Own transportation and references req'd. Leave message. 555-0986.

Nanny—Needed M–F 6 A.M.–4 P.M. Experience and references required. 555-2163 after 6 P.M.

WHAT BEING A NANNY IS LIKE

Nannies are not baby-sitters; they are highly trained professionals who take care of children in a family home. Most nannies are female; however, there are a few male nannies. According to the International Nanny Association, nannies are child care specialists who care for children in a family home. They may work full time or part time and may or may not live with the family. As loving, nurturing, and trustworthy companions to children, they play a vital role in the family support system.

The International Nanny Association has adopted minimum standards for nannies specifying that a nanny must be at least 18 years of age, have completed high school or the equivalent, and be in good general health, with proof of negative tuberculosis test and/or chest x-ray. The one qualification that all nannies must also have is genuine respect for and devotion to children.

APTITUDES

Nannies may work for families who are quite different from their own. Their work hours may be quite long and the work very arduous. According to the International Nanny Association, nannies need to have the following capabilities in order to handle the job effectively:

- The ability to work in isolation without the support of coworkers
- The ability to handle new and different surroundings
- Knowledge of the basics of taking care of the physical and emotional needs of infants and young children
- The ability to handle an emergency
- Basic knowledge of child development
- Good communication skills
- The ability to be organized

Families expect nannies to have no history of alcohol or drug abuse and a safe driving record and almost always prefer a nanny who does not smoke. And of course, it certainly helps if a nanny has a sense of humor.

A NANNY'S JOB DESCRIPTION

The job description for a nanny will obviously vary from household to household. In general, nannies have the following responsibilities, according to the International Nanny Association:

- Tending to the child's basic daily physical needs
- Meal planning and preparation
- Laundry and clothing care

- Organization of play activities and outings

- Discipline

- Intellectual stimulation

- Language activities

- Transportation

Any housekeeping responsibilities nannies may have are related primarily to the care of the children.

THE TYPICAL DAY OF A NANNY

One way to understand how nannies spend their time on the job is to look at the schedule of a nanny entrusted to care for three young children—Mary (7), John (5), and Larry (3):

7:00 A.M.   Start work.

7:05 A.M.   See that Mary gets on the school bus.

7:30 A.M.–9:00 A.M.   Feed the boys. See that they get dressed. Children then watch television. Help John with kindergarten speech. The children help clean up the house.

9:00 A.M.–10:30 A.M.   Go to the park first, and then to the library to choose books.

10:30 A.M.–11:00 A.M.   Prepare lunch for the boys. Make sure John is ready for kindergarten.

11:00 A.M. – 12:30 P.M.   Feed the children. Walk John to kindergarten.

12:30 P.M.–2:30 P.M.   Read to Larry. Larry rests. Do laundry and other household tasks.

2:30 P.M.–3:00 P.M.   Visit with Mary, who has returned from school.

3:00 P.M.   John returns home. Serve afternoon snack to children.

3:30 P.M.–4:30 P.M.   The children do their chores and homework. Mary practices piano.

4:30 P.M. The children play during the next two hours with some supervision. Dinner is prepared.

6:30 P.M. Family meal.

7:00 P.M. Day is finished.

SALARY AND FRINGE BENEFITS

Nannies are the elite of child care workers and are enjoying rising wages. The Delta College Nanny Program reports that nanny positions have a salary range of $400 to $600 a week, with an average starting salary of $450 a week. The actual salary that a nanny receives does vary widely based on where the nanny lives and the nanny's qualifications and experience. In addition to a salary, many nannies receive paid health insurance, room and board, a car to drive, travel to exotic vacation spots, membership in health clubs, and an opportunity to attend college part time. Some families even pay college tuition for their nannies. Nannies with a college education in high demand areas may earn up to $40,000 and $50,000 a year.

TRAINING AND OTHER QUALIFICATIONS

The International Nanny Association strongly supports specialized training for nannies who care for children in an in-home setting. Prospective nannies should contact this international network of nannies, nanny placement agency owners, nanny educators, and nanny employers for career information. Contact the International Nanny Association at Station House, Suite 438, 900 Haddon Avenue, Collingswood, NJ 08108, or visit their website at www.nanny.org.

Required Competencies Through education nannies can acquire the competencies needed to provide quality child care and a nurturing environment for all children. The International Nanny Association specifically recommends that a nanny demonstrate the ability to perform competently in the following areas:

- Observe and assess the behavior of children

- Plan and implement consistent daily routines

- Create an environment to foster trust, self-esteem, and independence in children

- Use age-appropriate behavior management techniques in interaction with children

- Plan and implement developmentally appropriate play/learning activities for children

- Choose and care for developmentally appropriate play materials and equipment

Competencies related to interaction with parents/employers and to family dynamics:

- Communicate effectively, both orally and in writing

- Articulate a personal philosophy of child care

- Maintain the confidentiality of the employing family

- Demonstrate knowledge and understanding of parents'/employer's philosophy of child rearing and recognize the special role a nanny assumes in becoming a part of the child-rearing "team"

- Recognize the ultimate authority of parents in making decisions regarding the welfare and care of the child

- Follow instructions and directions in a timely manner

Competencies related to professionalism, personal development, and social skills:

- Present a professional attitude and appearance

- Use good judgment

- Use appropriate language and manners

- Demonstrate initiative in planning and performance of tasks and an ability to work unsupervised

- Participate in social, cultural, and educational activities to enhance personal growth and maintain and improve competency

Competencies related to the physical care of children:

- Perform tasks related to the physical care of children

- Maintain appropriate hygienic standards for children regarding bathing, hand washing, and care of the hair and teeth

- Feed, change, and bathe infants

- Prepare infant feedings and care for feeding equipment

- Select clothing appropriate to the child's physical/social activities

- Plan and supervise rest, bed, and nap times

- Plan and prepare nutritionally balanced meals and snacks

- Care for the mildly ill child

- Recognize symptoms of common childhood illnesses

- Keep accurate records

- Perform appropriate first-aid techniques

- Handle emergency situations

- Observe appropriate safety precautions when traveling with children

Competencies related to domestic tasks and care of the child's environment:

- Perform domestic tasks related to care and maintenance of the child's areas of the home such as bedrooms, playrooms, bathrooms, and outside play space

- Launder and make simple repairs to children's clothing

- Observe safety precautions appropriate to a private home

Nanny Training Programs

There are several approaches to acquiring the formal training nannies need. Some nannies obtain associate's or bachelor's degrees in early childhood education. Many attend training programs in private schools, vocational schools, and community colleges. Typical nanny training programs offer a variety of courses related to children and child care. There are courses in child growth and development, psychology, food and nutrition, health and safety, play activities, first aid, cardiopulmonary resuscitation (CPR), and family dynamics. The programs often include hands-on care of children. Many schools provide the future nanny with information on personal health and grooming, etiquette, social skills, and professional development.

A Public College Program

Vincennes University in Vincennes, Indiana, has a professional nanny program. The program is a one-year, certificate degree program and requires completion of 32 credit hours. Figure 4.1 shows the actual curriculum as it appears in the college catalog. The program has been accredited by the American Council of Nanny Schools.

As part of the curriculum, each student spends a total of 240 hours in the community working with children. Sites include day care centers, nursery schools, YMCA programs, Head Start programs, a hospital pediatric unit, a university day care center, and many private homes. The students are monitored by site supervisors, personnel, and the coordinator of the Vincennes University Professional Nanny Program.

Figure 4.1   Curriculum for Professional Nanny Program

**Professional Nanny
Certificate Option**

Intensive training program for the Child Care Professional who will enter a family's home and share in the responsibility of rearing their children.

    The Child Care Professional Nanny Certificate Program prepares students to meet the varied needs of the families they serve and integrate their lives with those of their employers. These duties could include adapting menus to special dietary needs, managing the day-to-day affairs of the household, aiding a handicapped or gifted child, and communicating with schools, parents, and children. (1)

Semester I

HHH	130	Infant, Toddler, and Child Care	3
HMM	117	Fundamentals of Music (2)	2
HHH	210	Food Preparation (3)	3
HHH	211	Food Preparation and Nutrition Lab	1
HHH	156	Marriage and Family (2)	3
HHH	140	Field Placement I	2
HHH	141	Field Placement Seminar I	1
PPE		Physical Education Elective (3)	1
			16

Semester II

APS	142	General Psychology	3
HAH	104	Design and Materials (2)	3
HHH	132	The Nanny as a Professional	1
HHH	137	Home Management and Family Communications	3
PHE	111	First Aid (3)	2
PPE		Physical Education Elective (3)	1
HHH	142	Field Placement II	2
HHH	143	Field Placement Seminar II	1
			16

(1) The Child Care Professional Nanny will meet the standards set by the American Council of Nanny Schools Incorporated, and the program will be accredited by the ACNS. Upon successful completion of 32 semester hours of specified courses, the student will receive a certificate of accreditation as a Child Care Professional Nanny from Vincennes University.

(2) Students who wish to continue their education find that the Child Care Professional Nanny certificate is the first step in their career ladder. These credits received at Vincennes University can be applied toward an associate's degree. This training can often be applied toward degrees that allow the certificate candidate to move on toward degrees in teaching or other child care professions.

(3) It is highly recommended that students achieve Red Cross life saving certification or intermediate swimming proficiency.

**Nanny School
Courses**

The following are descriptions of some of the courses taken by prospective nannies in the Vincennes University Professional Nanny Program.

HHH 210 Food Preparation. 3 hours (Sem I). The basic principles involved in the preparation of food are both studied and applied. 2 lecture hours, 4 laboratory hours.

HHH 211 Food Preparation and Nutrition Lab. 1 hour (Sem I). A course designed for the child care professional nanny certificate student. Proper preparation of foods, food sanitation, healthy snacks, and the meeting of the nutritional requirements of children with special needs will be emphasized. 2 lecture/laboratory hours.

HHH 130 Infant, Toddler, and Child Care. 3 hours (Sem I). Principles and philosophy of infant, toddler, and child care. Social, emotional, mental, and physical development from birth to adolescence as it relates to the care of infants, toddlers, and children is examined. Additional topics include safety concerns, special needs of children, and community resources. 3 lecture/laboratory hours.

HHH 132 The Nanny as a Professional. 1 hour (Sem II). An introductory but comprehensive course concerning the nanny as a professional, including professionalism, ethics, confidentiality, employer/employee relations, occupational communications, contracts and the law, wages and benefits, social graces, and personal development. 1 lecture hour.

HHH 137 Home Management and Family Communications. 3 hours (Sem II). A study of home management techniques and family communication skills with emphasis on practical application. Home management topics include maintenance, time management, safety and security issues, household problems, emergencies, clothing care, and consumer issues. Family communication topics include conflict resolution, family relations, impact of media, special needs of children, and social factors affecting family life. 3 lecture hours.

HHH 140 Field Placement I. 2 hours (Sem I). Practical experience in child care settings working with infants, toddlers, and children under the supervision of experienced teachers and child care personnel. Placements involve caring for infants, toddlers, and preschoolers nine hours per week, for a total of at least 120 clock hours per semester. Sites include the Vincennes University Day Care, YMCA Day Care, Head Start, and others. 9 field experience hours.

HHH 141 Field Placement Seminar I. 1 hour (Sem I). To be taken concurrently with HHH 140. An in-depth analysis of the field placement experience. A study of teaching principles, practices, and techniques appropriate to the needs of the young child. Materials and learning experiences in language, storytelling, music, art, and motor skills as well as exploration of community resources are included. 1 lecture hour.

HHH 142 Field Placement II. 2 hours (Sem II). Practical experience in child care under the supervision of caregivers and a Vincennes UniversityCenter, faculty member. Placement rotations build on the skills and experiences acquired in Field Placement I. Sites include homes and day care facilities. The course offers the students responsibilities similar to those of the nanny profession. 9 field experience hours.

HHH 143 Field Placement Seminar II. 1 hour (Sem II). To be taken concurrently with HHH 142. A continuation of in-depth study of methods and materials. 1 lecture hour.

CHOOSING A NANNY SCHOOL

A listing of nanny training schools can be obtained by contacting the American Council of Nanny Schools, Office A74, Delta College, University Center, MI 48710. The International Nanny Association publishes the *Directory of Nanny Training Programs, Placement Agencies and Special Services*. The book's section on schools has information about the length of training programs, program costs, admission requirements, and availability of financial aid for schools that meet the association's requirements.

Because the career of professional nanny is relatively new in the United States, there are not yet any national standards for training programs, nor are there national credentials to certify that a nanny has achieved a certain level of knowledge and expertise.

Before enrolling in a nanny school, prospective nannies should carefully check out the merits of the school's program, according to Joy Shelton, the chairperson of the American Council of Nanny Schools. She offers the following suggestions on how a program should be assessed:

• Talk to graduates

• Talk to families that have hired students from the school

• Check with the Better Business Bureau and local chamber of commerce to make sure that no complaints about the school have been received

• Check with the state's department of education to determine if the school has a license

• Find out if the school is accredited

The International Nanny Association lists these questions for prospective nannies to ask about a training program:

1. What specific courses does the nanny program curriculum include?

2. If the program requires work with children as part of the training, is the work supervised by an instructor?

3. Is the program accredited by a federally approved accrediting body?

4. What are the qualifications of the instructors?

5. How many students have completed the training program? Were they able to find jobs as nannies?

6. Is it possible to visit the school or sit in on a class?

7. What is the tuition refund policy if the student drops out of the course? Can the course work be transferred to another school or program?

8. Is counseling or tutoring available to the student who may be having trouble with the program?

9. What percentage of students who sign up for the program complete it?

Recommended competencies for the education of nannies are available from the International Nanny Association office upon request.

APPLYING TO A NANNY SCHOOL

Nanny schools are looking for candidates who have the backgrounds, interests, and experiences that will enable them to become excellent nannies after training. Delta College Nanny Program uses a screening process to make sure that enrollees do not have a criminal record or their name on a child abuse registry. In addition, the college is looking for candidates with an above-average driving record, a clean drug and alcohol record, and no medical disabilities that would prevent them in any way from caring for their charges. Physically, they should be able to stoop, kneel, crouch, and crawl. Good vision and hearing are necessary, as well as being able to lift 50 pounds. On the personality side, the college wants prospective students to demonstrate creativity, time management skills, initiative, responsibility, self-confidence, and a love of teaching and children. On page 52 is an announcement describing the Delta College Nanny Program. Other nanny schools have similar admissions requirements.

NANNY CODE OF CONDUCT

The International Nanny Association has adopted a Code of Conduct to promote professionalism and ethical practices among nannies, educators, and those who employ and place in-home child care specialists. By virtue of their membership in the International Nanny Association, members agree to abide by this Code of Conduct and to support quality in-home child care for the world's most valuable resources—our children.

Delta College
COMMUNITY SERVICES
NANNY PROGRAM Fall, 1999

WE NEED YOU!

Become a Certified Professional Nanny by graduating from this American
Council of Nanny Schools accredited program. You will be joining an elite
group of child care providers who have earned the privilege to work with
children. Work in an environment where your professionalism is appreciated and valued, earn generous salaries with full benefits, meet new and
interesting people, travel to exciting destinations, and see the world through
the eyes of a child. Thousands of jobs available locally and nationwide.

The demand for Nannies is much greater than the number of persons trained.
Join this new profession by enrolling today in one of the following Nanny
Programs.

- **Daytime Program** – Five days a week. Classes and fieldwork
  — One Semester
  CFA1200-01 • Staff • Mon.–Fri. • 9/7-12/14 • 8 A.M.–4 P.M.

- **Evening Program**
  CFA1212-01 • Staff • Mon., Tues., Thur.
  9/13/99-2/17/00 • 6–10 P.M.

FEES: $1,428 In-District; $1,764 Out-District; $2,308 Out-State; $964
Senior Citizens

NANNY COURSE WORK INCLUDES:

- Creative Activities with Children
- Physical Care of Infants & Children
- Building Effective Relationships
- Nutrition
- Child Development I
- Professional Development for Nannies
- Child Development II
- Practicum as a Nanny
- Study of Family Dynamics

Upon successful completion of course work, a certificate will be awarded.

TO REGISTER:

To Register: Mail or bring in completed registration form along
with full payment or call (517) 686-9427 with Visa or
MasterCard.

For Info Call: Delta College, Community Services
(517) 686-9470 or (517) 686-9417
Midland: (517) 495-4000, ext. 9470 or 9417

Responsibilities to the Child
A nanny shall:

- Respect each child as a human being and never knowingly participate in any practice that is disrespectful, dangerous, exploitive, intimidating, or psychologically or physically harmful.

- Maintain a safe and healthy atmosphere that encourages optimum social, emotional, intellectual, and physical development of children.

- Provide various learning opportunities through which a child can explore and utilize his or her continued personal growth and development.

- Recognize the unique potential of each child, encourage questions, and present answers that children can understand.

- Keep abreast of current activity in the areas of childhood development through continued education, either formally or informally.

- Work toward promoting knowledge and understanding of young children and their needs and act as an advocate for children's rights.

- Be familiar with the signs of child abuse and neglect and be knowledgeable of procedures for dealing with them.

Responsibilities to the Parents
A nanny shall:

- Treat parents and other family members with respect by maintaining confidentiality and respecting the family's right to privacy.

- Work together with parents to create an environment conducive to the healthy development of the child.

- Respect the family's child-rearing values and parents' rights to make decisions for their children.

- Support the family value system, cultural expression, and individual characteristics and refrain from imposing personal values or biases upon the child.

- Be an advocate for children and work to protect their rights.

- Not hold the child accountable for negative interactions between parents and nanny.

- Inform parents of physical injury, illness, and emotional crises should they occur in the child's life.

Responsibilities to Self
A nanny shall:

- Present herself/himself as an acceptable adult role model, take pride in personal appearance and professional behavior, and refrain from activity that might injure credibility or produce a negative representation of herself/himself or an employer.

- Continue to improve personal knowledge of child development by seeking contemporary information through formal and informal means, such as membership in child care organizations.

FINDING EMPLOYMENT AS A NANNY

Nannies can find jobs through newspaper advertisements and referrals from friends. However, the International Nanny Association suggests that nannies rely on their training school placement bureaus and nanny placement agencies to avoid negative experiences. Placement agencies match the nanny's qualifications and preferences with the needs of families searching for nannies. The family, not the nanny, is charged for the placement service.

A nanny agency typically requires nannies to complete an application, supply references, and have an interview with agency personnel. According to the International Nanny Association, this process may also involve taking fingerprints and checking to see whether the nanny has a criminal record or bad driving record. The prospective nanny may also be required to take a blood test and tuberculosis test and may be requested to provide a physician's statement certifying that the nanny is in good health and free of contagious diseases. It is also essential to prove United States citizenship or eligibility to work legally in this country.

Working with a Placement Agency

Indy Nannies Plus is a midwestern nanny placement agency. Since the agency was started in 1991, it has had thousands of calls from clients interested in hiring nannies, which attests to the great demand for nannies. Indy Nannies Plus acts as a go-between, screening both clients and nannies to get the perfect fit. At no cost to the nanny, the agency will give the nanny a physical exam, a tuberculosis test, and a drug test; in addition, the agency will arrange for fingerprint, criminal background, and driving record checks and will train the nanny in CPR.

To be eligible for placement by the agency, nannies need to have two years of child care experience or a two-year associate's degree. If this requirement is met, and after satisfactorily completing preliminary applications, the nanny will fill out the application shown in Figure 4.2.

The agency also requires all nannies to write a "Dear Parent" letter (see page 57) to introduce themselves to parents who might wish to interview them. The following letter was written by a prospective nanny named Linette:

Figure 4.2   Nanny Agency Application

Application

Please type or print clearly.   Date _____

PERSONAL INFORMATION   Referral Source _____

Name _____Social Security #_____

Home Address_____ Phone #_____

City _____ State_____Zip_____

Are you 18 years or older?_____   Drivers License #_____

EMPLOYMENT DESIRED

                                                Date you   Salary
Position_____ can start_____ desired_____

Do you desire: Full-time_____   Part-time_____

Summer Only_____   Live-In_____   Live-Out _____

EDUCATION

List high schools, colleges, or other training.

Name/Location	Dates Attended	Graduate?	Major

GENERAL

Special Skills_____

Hobbies/Interests_____

Are you certified in CPR/First Aid?_____ When_____

PLEASE COMPLETE THE BACK OF THIS APPLICATION

Figure 4.2   Nanny Agency Application (continued)

FORMER EMPLOYERS

List below last four employers, starting with last one.

Name/Location	Dates From-To	Position	Reason for Leaving

REFERENCES

Give the names of three persons not related to you, whom you have known at least one year.

Name	Address	Phone	Years Known

List all child care experience:_____

_____

Please read the following carefully; sign and date.

I certify that the facts contained in this application are true and complete to the best of my knowledge and understand that, if employed, falsified statements on this application will cancel placement.

I authorize investigation of all statements contained herein and the references listed above to give you any and all information concerning my previous employment and any pertinent information they may have, and release all parties from all liability for any damages that may result from furnishing same to you.

I understand and agree that, if hired, my employment is for no definite period and may, regardless of the date of payment of my wages and salary, be terminated at any time without prior notice and without cause.

Date_____   Signature_____

Dear Parent,

Hi, my name is Linette. I am a 24-year-old single female with caring, honest, and reliable attributes. I am laid-back and flexible and try to possess an open mind at all times. Some of my interests include working out, walking, reading, and participating in outdoor activities. I have learned to be very creative when it comes to free time. I am always eager to try new activities and have a desire to learn. I am hoping to obtain a live-in nanny position in which two or three toddlers are involved. I prefer ages 1 and above but would not turn down an opportunity in which an infant was involved.

I recently received my B.S. in sociology with a minor in criminal justice. I graduated in December 20__ from Iowa State University in Ames, Iowa. During my studies at Iowa State, I had the opportunity to enroll in child development classes. I learned a lot about toddlers and the different stages of development they go through. I truly enjoyed these classes, and I am hoping to pursue a career involving toddlers. My future plans include returning to college to obtain my master's degree in early childhood or family and marriage counseling.

My work history has allowed me to gain valuable experience. I have learned to work as a team member and how to accept responsibility for my own actions. My communication skills have improved due to the amount of interaction I have had with various people. Employers and coworkers have often complimented me on my ability to be efficient, confident, and dependable. Although my job experiences do not directly involve children, I feel you will be able to develop a good idea of what kind of employee I would be. As far as experience with children, I come from a family with five brothers and six sisters. I fall right in the middle. Therefore, I have had lots of experience with my six younger brothers and sisters. During grade school and high school, I have also had various baby-sitting jobs. I would be more than happy to provide you with the names of these people. With all this behind me, I feel I am well qualified for commitment to your family.

I sincerely hope you will consider me for an interview with you and your family. I strongly believe I will be a positive role model for your children.

Thank you for your time and consideration.

Interviewing for a Nanny Position

Part of the process of obtaining a nanny position is being interviewed by prospective employers. The Indy Nannies Plus agency holds interviews in which clients talk to nannies selected by the agency. Each interview is scheduled for approximately 30 minutes. Here is a list of the questions that parents are given to help them interview nannies:

1. What is your best quality?

2. Are you flexible?

3. Are you punctual?

4. What is your approach to discipline?

5. How many children do you feel comfortable caring for?

6. What ages of children do you prefer?

7. Tell me about your experiences with children. What did you like most? Least?

8. How long of a commitment can you make?

9. How assertive are you?

10. Are you willing to care for children according to my philosophies?

11. What are some of the activities you would like to do with children?

12. If you took them on field trips, where would you like to go?

13. How do you react to criticism?

14. Tell me about your background.

15. Do you know how to childproof a home?

16. Do you know the Heimlich maneuver?

17. Do you feel comfortable driving with children in the car?

18. What hours can you work?

19. Can you work overtime? Weekends? Travel with our family on vacation?

20. What are your feelings about doing light housework?

21. What do you consider light housework to be?

22. Why do you want to be a nanny?

23. How many days did you miss from your job last year?

At this agency clients usually find a nanny from the first group of interviews. If not, three additional nannies will be chosen for interviews. The agency always suggests that a second interview be held in the client's home so the client can see how the nanny interacts with the children. The agency advises both clients and nannies that if either has any apprehension about the other, no commitments should be made. If a perfect match is made, both nanny and client return to the office to negotiate a contract. It is important that both parties understand the job. Everything must be spelled out clearly in the contract. The contract shown in Figure 4.3 demonstrates what is involved in nanny/client contracts.

The agency gives its clients a 30-day trial period. If the relationship between nanny and family does not work out during this time, Indy Nannies Plus will locate a new home for the nanny and a new nanny for the family.

THE AU PAIR EXPERIENCE

Nannies are take-charge people who are completely responsible for the care of children. Au pairs also live with families and provide help with child care and

Figure 4.3   Employer/Nanny Contract

EMPLOYER/NANNY

This agreement is entered into between_____

(employer)

and_____.

(nanny)

The employer seeks to secure the nanny as a professional child caregiver, and nanny wishes to provide such services.

Employer's Address_____ Telephone_____

_____ Zip Code_____

Employer's Child(ren) Name_____ Age_____

Name_____ Age_____

Name_____ Age_____

Nanny's Address_____ Telephone_____

_____ Zip Code_____

Nanny's Social Security Number_____

Nanny's Compensation: Salary_____ /Hrly_____

Overtime Pay_____ Holiday Pay_____

Scheduled Hours_____ Days_____

Nanny is to receive_____ Vacation Days

Paid Vacation Yes_____ No_____   Paid Holidays Yes_____ No_____

Nanny is to receive the following holidays _____

_____

DUTIES:

Child Care_____

Household_____

Errands_____

Transporting_____

Other _____

TERMINATION:

Nanny agrees to pay the employer $_____ if the nanny quits before

_____. The nanny will give_____weeks notice prior

to leaving employment. Employer will give nanny _____weeks notice and

$_____severance pay to terminate agreement.

Nanny's Signature_____ Date_____

Employer's Signature_____ Date_____

light housework. They usually work under the direct supervision of the parent and may or may not have previous child care experience. Au pairs will work from 40 to 60 hours a week. Besides American au pairs, there are foreign au pairs who live in the United States for up to a year to experience American life. They live as part of the host family and receive a small allowance/salary in exchange for help with child care and housework. Americans can also work abroad as au pairs, usually in Europe, to experience the culture of another country.

THE REWARDS OF BEING A NANNY

The care of children in a home setting can be a rewarding career. Nannies are able to provide children with the nurturing care they need; in return, the nannies will receive love and affection from the children as well as high regard from their families. Today's nannies provide the high quality in-home care that parents are seeking and receive respect as well-trained professionals.

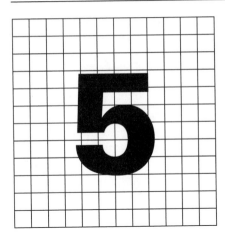

BABY-SITTING CAREER OPPORTUNITIES

Many who now have careers working with children first worked in this area as baby-sitters. While most baby-sitters are teenagers, many are adults who work in the children's home or their own homes on a part-time or full-time basis. There is a very high demand for and low supply of baby-sitters, especially for special occasions.

Even though there are no licensing or training requirements for this job, the more skilled baby-sitters are, the more clients they have, and the more money they earn. Well-qualified baby-sitters know the importance of learning all they can about taking care of children. They must be ready to perform cardiopulmonary resuscitation (CPR) in an emergency, handle a child with a sore throat, or treat a sprained finger. These skills are learned through classes at YMCAs or YWCAs, high schools, vocational schools, and community colleges, and through the American Red Cross.

ACQUIRING BABY-SITTING SKILLS

Child care classes provide practical training in health and safety and important information about child development. They provide instruction on how to prevent injuries and reduce the spread of infectious diseases. In these classes, baby-sitters and other child care providers learn how to recognize and care for common childhood illnesses. They also find out how to improve their skills in communicating with children and their parents.

The American Red Cross has produced, in cooperation with the American Academy of Pediatrics and with review from the National Academy of Sciences, the first and only national program designed for child care providers. The child care course is taught by a certified instructor who presents the information in an easy-to-follow format through group discussions, videos, demonstrations, role playing, and short lectures. At the conclusion of the course, a handy, attractive workbook is given to participants to serve as a ready resource when they are caring for young children.

The Red Cross presents their child care course in seven units:

1. Preventing Childhood Injuries

2. Infant and Child First Aid

3. Caring for Ill Children

4. Preventing Infectious Diseases

5. Learning About Child Development

6. Communicating with Children and Parents

7. Recognizing and Reporting Child Abuse

The Red Cross also has a baby-sitting course designed especially for those who will be watching children on a part-time or irregular basis. It consists of six parts:

1. The responsibilities of a baby-sitter

2. How to interview for a job

3. What to expect of parents

4. What parents expect the baby-sitter to do

5. How to market yourself safely

6. How to perform first aid, prevent injuries, and handle emergencies

Taking classes and learning how to care for children is no guarantee that a prospective baby-sitter will be an excellent one. Certain special qualifications are needed. Baby-sitters need to have patience to play endless games with children. They should truly enjoy being around children, whether the children are crying babies or rambunctious youngsters. Furthermore, baby-sitters need to be confident that they can handle children ranging in age from infant to preteen. Finally, having a cool head in a crisis is an absolutely essential skill, as baby-sitters must remain calm in emergencies.

BABY-SITTERS NEED TO KNOW HOW CHILDREN DEVELOP

Every child has a unique timetable that determines at what age he or she will walk, talk, and dress independently. At the same time, general guidelines describe when children typically acquire most skills. Baby-sitters need to know what their young charges should be expected to do so they can plan age-appropriate activities. The following skills checklists were developed by the authors and first published by Meadowbrook Press in *Ready for School? What Every Preschooler Should Know.*

**Checklist of Expected
Listening Skills**

Birth to 15 months

- Reacts differently to loud and soft sounds
- Looks to see where sounds come from
- Responds to human voices
- Knows the difference between angry and happy
- Identifies different speakers
- Likes to listen to self babble or talk
- Knows the sounds that favorite toys make
- Imitates sounds
- Recognizes own name
- Understands names of familiar people and objects
- Begins to respond to commands
- Understands more words than can actually say
- Associates sounds with objects (drums, rattles)
- Understands "no"
- Enjoys listening to poems and stories

By 2¹/₂ years

- Likes to be read to
- Has favorite storybooks
- Listens to short stories
- Recognizes the words for common objects
- Recognizes the names of people
- Identifies body parts
- Understands the position words *on, under, in*
- Understands simple questions
- Understands simple commands
- Listens for the meanings of words, not just sounds
- Listens to adult conversations
- Repeats sounds, words, and phrases

By 5 years

- Appreciates stories, poems, and music
- Listens to stories without interruption
- Recalls story facts
- Retells a simple story in sequence
- Tells the meanings of words heard in a story
- Repeats simple nursery rhymes
- Follows simple two- and three-step commands
- Understands and follows rules
- Recognizes common sounds (animals, cars, running water)
- Distinguishes between loud and soft sounds
- Identifies beginning sounds of words
- Hears the differences between similar sounds
- Identifies rhyming sounds
- Copies simple rhythmic patterns (clap clap—clap clap)
- Imitates common sounds (dog, siren, horn)
- Hears soft whispers and understands the words
- Identifies unfamiliar words and asks their meanings
- Tells the meanings of simple words
- Understands the position words *in front of, behind, toward*
- Understands most adult sentences
- Repeats a series of five numbers
- Plays games such as Simon Says

Checklist of Expected Thinking Skills

Birth to 15 months

- Reaches and grasps objects intentionally
- Recognizes objects and people
- Is aware of basic body parts
- Uses all five senses to gain information
- Is aware that certain events follow other events (crying brings parents)
- Performs an action to see the effect (drops object on the floor for someone to pick up)
- Imitates play of others

By 2¹/₂ years

- Learns and expects routine

- Sees similarities and differences in objects and people

- Groups similar objects on the basis of one characteristic

- Relies on senses to gain information

- Shows some control of the environment (turns off faucets, shuts off lights)

- Understands that events can be sequenced

- Recalls recent events

- Expects absent people or objects to reappear at appropriate time or place

- Begins to solve problems and make decisions

By 5 years

- Recognizes similarities and differences in shapes, patterns, and figures

- Copies simple shapes (square, circle, triangle)

- Identifies missing parts in pictures

- Maintains attention on adult-directed tasks for short periods of time

- Maintains attention on own tasks for longer periods of time

- Practices to gain mastery of tasks

- Gets information by observing and asking questions

- Begins to link past and present information

- Begins to develop simple memory strategies

- Begins to recognize differences between the real world and fantasy

- Realizes actions have both a cause and effect

- Makes simple generalizations

- Groups objects on the basis of one or more characteristics

- Tells what happened first, second, and third

- Shows understanding of general times of day (morning, noon, night)

- Knows colors

Checklist of Expected Fine Motor Skills

Birth to 15 months

- Uses reaching and holding reflexes

- Puts objects in hands and mouth

- Picks up objects with a palm grasp

- Grasps and releases an object

- Handles objects with either hand

- Transfers object from one hand to the other

- Likes manipulating small objects

- Uses spoon as tool to bring food to his/her mouth

- Uses one finger to poke or push an object

- Tears paper

- Stacks blocks

- Uses thumb and forefinger

- Crams many objects into hands

- Turns pages in a book

By 2¹/₂ years

- Uses a palm grasp when scribbling

- Uses thumb and forefinger to grasp an object

- Drinks out of a sipper cup

- Throws a large ball

- Shows a hand preference

- Uses a marker on paper

- Uses a pegboard

- Strings beads

- Squeezes a toy

- Turns knobs

- Works Velcro

- Handles snaps

- Screws on tops

By 5 years

- Manipulates small objects with both hands

- Builds with building toys

- Kneads dough

- Cuts with scissors
- Holds crayons appropriately
- Colors a picture
- Draws a person with at least six body parts
- Traces, copies, and draws basic shapes
- Folds triangles from squares
- Copies a design
- Copies a letter
- Pastes objects on a piece of paper
- Cuts out simple shapes
- Writes numerals 1 to 15
- Uses a fork correctly
- Laces shoes
- Ties knots
- Buttons a coat
- Paints a picture
- Pounds in pegs with control
- Picks up and fits objects together with ease
- Pours liquid into a glass without spilling
- Puts a 10-piece puzzle together
- Makes shadow shapes on the wall
- Spreads peanut butter on a piece of bread

Checklist of Expected Social Skills

Birth to 15 months

- Waves bye-bye
- Imitates behavior of parents and caretakers
- Responds to or imitates games such as Pat-a-Cake
- Anticipates feeding, dressing, and bathing
- Distinguishes between familiar people and strangers
- Adapts to changing people and places
- Shows considerable interest in peers

- Enjoys exploring objects with another person
- Gets others to do things for his/her pleasure
- Gives and takes objects

By 2¹/₂ years

- Imitates behavior of peers and adults
- Plays alongside another child
- Calls some children friends
- Enjoys small group activities for short periods of time
- Starts to see benefits of cooperation
- Has some awareness of the feelings of others
- Shows some control of impulses in dealing with others
- Starts to recognize that others have rights and privileges
- Begins to assert self appropriately in some situations

By 5 years

- Approaches new people with interest
- Begins to show awareness of similarities and differences among people
- Begins to have empathy for others
- Begins to function as a group member
- Uses play to explore social roles
- Manages peer conflict constructively
- Begins to share with others
- Starts to take turns
- Functions as a leader or follower in play situations
- Does not interfere with the work of others
- Asserts rights appropriately
- Begins to follow rules
- Recognizes authority
- Makes appropriate social responses
- Seeks help when needed

Checklist of Expected Self-Help Skills

Birth to 15 months

- Has developed senses
- Looks at a body part when it is touched
- Places objects in hands
- Clasps hands and fingers together
- Begins to use a spoon

By 2¹/₂ years

- Attempts to go to the bathroom without help
- Washes hands
- Combs hair
- Brushes teeth
- Puts on socks
- Puts on shoes
- Feeds self

By 5 years

- Completes toilet skills
- Dresses and undresses self completely
- Washes face and hands
- Knows how to use a handkerchief or tissue
- Fastens buckles
- Buttons shirts, pants, and coats
- Zips zippers
- Opens and closes snaps
- Puts on boots
- Puts on gloves or mittens
- Uses a spoon or fork effectively
- Uses a knife for spreading
- Pours a drink

- Takes toys out to play with them
- Puts toys away

**Checklist of Expected
Self-Esteem Skills**

Birth to 15 months

- Shows intense feelings for parents
- Shows affection for familiar person through hugs and smiles
- Shows pride and pleasure in mastering tasks
- Expresses clearly differentiated emotions such as pleasure, disappointment, anger, fear, joy, and excitement
- Puts self to sleep
- Begins to quiet self
- Asserts self

By 2¹/₂ years

- Differentiates facial expressions of anger, sadness, and joy
- Demonstrates awareness of own feelings
- Demonstrates awareness of others' feelings
- Expresses feeling through dramatic play
- Verbalizes feelings
- Shows increased control of emotions
- Begins to sense what is acceptable and unacceptable behavior
- Shows pride in new accomplishments
- Begins to appreciate own competency
- Has emerging sense of self

By 5 years

- Begins to recognize and label emotions such as anger, happiness, sadness, and fear
- Expresses both positive and negative feelings
- Has knowledge of own gender and ethnic background
- Has initiative to try new things
- Acts confident in new situations

- Makes decisions
- Postpones gratification
- Begins to exercise self-control
- Is not easily frustrated
- Does not cry easily
- Displays even temper
- Understands the idea of acceptable behavior
- Does not require constant support from parents or caregivers
- Separates from parents without being upset
- Starts to understand own strengths and limitations
- Has strong and positive sense of self

Checklist of Expected Speaking Skills

Birth to 15 months

- Coos and gurgles in infancy
- Repeats same sounds frequently
- Cries differently for different needs
- Babbles, using different sounds
- Uses voice to get attention
- Uses voice to establish social contact
- Enjoys imitating sounds
- Enjoys making sounds of familiar animals and objects
- Laughs a lot
- Says a few words such as "mama" and "dada"

By 2½ years

- Uses more words than gestures
- Asks questions
- Responds to simple questions
- Repeats requests
- Names pictures
- Forms some plurals

• Uses two- and three-word sentences ("Eat cookie")

• Carries on conversation with self and dolls

• Refers to self by name

• Begins to verbalize some feelings

• Participates in conversations

By 5 years

• Produces understandable speech

• Labels familiar objects, people, and actions

• Defines objects by use (you drink from a glass)

• Uses descriptive words (large, good, cute)

• Uses the same sentence structure as family members

• Speaks in complete sentences

• Uses sentences of five to six words

• Asks questions for information

• Gives commands

• Varies intensity and tone of voice appropriately

• Sings simple songs

• Tells about recent personal experiences accurately

• Tells familiar stories

• Makes up pretend stories

Checklist of Expected Prereading Skills

Birth to 15 months

• Enjoys hearing stories, poems, and rhymes

• Enjoys looking at picture books

By 2^1/$_2$ years

• Shows preference for certain books

• Enjoys hearing stories, poems, and rhymes

• Retells stories

• Has the beginnings of a personal library

By 5 years

- Expresses self verbally

- Tells stories

- Looks at pictures and tells stories

- Repeats a sentence of six to eight words

- Answers questions about a short story

- Completes an incomplete sentence with the proper word

- Looks at books and magazines

- Enjoys hearing stories, poems, and rhymes

- Identifies rhyming words

- Knows some beginning sounds

- Makes fine visual discriminations

- Knows what an alphabet letter is

- Identifies some alphabet letters

- Recognizes some common sight words such as *stop*

- Pretends to read

- Understands print carries a message

- Understands the conventions of print

- Has a personal library

Checklist of Expected Math Skills

Birth to 15 months

- Judges the distance of an object from self correctly

- Uses all five senses to explore objects

- Identifies an object from different viewpoints

- Sees similarities in some objects

- Is aware that certain events regularly occur after others

By 2¹/₂ years

- Uses senses to gain information about objects

- Describes properties of objects (color, shape)

- Sees similarities and differences in objects

- Compares objects by size (big, little)
- Understands objects can be put in order (big, bigger)
- Understands events can be sequenced
- Begins to count objects in sequence (one ball, two balls)

By 5 years

- Recognizes likenesses and differences in shapes
- Sorts similar objects by color, size, and shape
- Matches objects based on shape
- Recognizes circles, squares, and triangles
- Copies simple shapes (circle, square, triangle)
- Understands concept of longest and shortest
- Understands concept of more and less
- Knows position words such as *on*, *behind*, *under*
- Counts objects in sequence to five (one ball, two balls)
- Recognizes groups of one to five objects
- Counts to five
- Arranges blocks in order by size

Checklist of Expected Gross Motor Skills

Birth to 15 months

- Lifts head
- Holds head up
- Sits without help
- Rolls over
- Crawls
- Crawls up stairs
- Crawls down stairs backward
- Pulls up to a standing position
- Balances on two feet
- Stands alone
- Takes a step

- Walks
- Walks and pushes an object
- Walks and carries a toy
- Throws an object

By 2¹/₂ years
- Walks on uneven surfaces
- Walks backward
- Walks up stairs using both feet and relying on support
- Climbs
- Starts to run
- Jumps off one step
- Rides small toy by pushing with feet
- Sits alone in a small chair
- Catches a ball
- Rolls a ball
- Pulls an object
- Copies simple movements

By 5 years
- Bends
- Walks a straight line
- Walks sideways
- Walks up and down stairs alternating feet
- Stands on tiptoes
- Walks on tiptoes
- Walks on low balance beam
- Marches
- Runs
- Jumps forward
- Jumps continuously

- Jumps backward

- Jumps and lands on both feet in one spot

- Jumps rope

- Skips

- Gallops

- Leaps

- Hops

- Stands on one foot with eyes open for five seconds

- Stands on one foot with eyes closed

- Drops and catches a ball

- Bounces a ball

- Kicks a ball

- Swings

- Pedals a tricycle or bicycle

THE BABY-SITTER'S RESPONSIBILITIES

Baby-sitters have several responsibilities from the moment they enter a home. Their major responsibility will be to watch the children, which includes:

- Playing with the children

- Preventing accidents

- Selecting safe and appropriate toys and games for each child

- Giving the children their undivided attention

- Changing diapers of infants and toddlers

- Bathing and dressing infants and young children

- Feeding babies

- Fixing meals or snacks for the children

- Cleaning up messes

- Handling the household

If a baby-sitting job is going to be long-term, the baby-sitter must meet with families ahead of time to establish their guidelines and expectations. On first-time assignments as well as subsequent jobs, baby-sitters need to secure five vital pieces of information before the parents leave:

1. General behavior guidelines

2. Rules on television viewing and snacking

3. The children's official bedtime

4. Special duties to be performed, such as bathing or feeding the children, doing dishes, etc.

5. A telephone number or information on how to reach the parents in case of an emergency

For all jobs, baby-sitters need to know where the following items are located in the home:

flashlight

candles

matches

first-aid kit

clock

cleaning supplies

sponge

vacuum cleaner

paper towels

writing paper

pencils, pens

tissues

telephone

thermostats

When baby-sitters watch children in their own homes, they have the additional responsibility of making their homes safe for children.

BABY-SITTERS NEED TO BE BUSINESSPEOPLE

Most baby-sitters find jobs through people they know or advertising their services on bulletin boards and in newspapers. Some baby-sitters work for agencies that will assign them to jobs. Baby-sitters need to discuss their fees and payment for extra services beyond routine child care before they begin to sit to avoid misunderstandings. Earnings are based on community standards. A baby-sitter in New York City or Chicago will earn more than one in rural North Dakota. Earnings are typically an hourly fee. However, older, experienced baby-sitters will be able to charge more for their services than their younger, less experienced counterparts.

HELPFUL HINTS FROM A BABY-SITTER

Jessica Donaldson, an eighth grader, has already been baby-sitting for more than three years. Starting at such a young age has become common because of the shortage of baby-sitters. Jessica does not establish a price with her clients. Instead, she feels that most people pay her a fair wage. She typically receives $4 an hour for baby-sitting for one child and more money for additional children. One family with three children pays her $5 an hour.

The families that hire Jessica to baby-sit expect her to keep the children out of trouble and to clean up any messes made by the children. Jessica believes that the major task in baby-sitting is to keep all the children entertained. She always asks families to provide her with specific information about how to reach them, when they will be home, and special directions for mealtimes, bedtimes, and any medications that need to be given.

Jessica has solid advice for prospective baby-sitters. She advises them to begin by going on a job with an experienced sitter to see what the job entails. Jessica believes that baby-sitters need to prepare for this job by learning how to change diapers and finding out what kind of things children of different ages like to do. Also, it is important to keep baby-sitting fun for both the sitter and the children so it does not become a routine and boring job. Jessica points out that the test of being a successful baby-sitter is being asked back again and again because the children love to have you.

BABY-SITTERS ARE IMPORTANT CAREGIVERS

Baby-sitters give parents worry-free workdays because they know their children are being carefully watched. They allow parents to have a few carefree hours of togetherness or a vacation without the company of their children. America's children need trained, well-qualified baby-sitters to help them grow and develop into healthy, happy people when their parents cannot be with them. Their job is important.

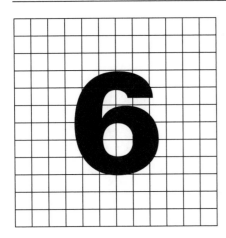

EDUCATION CAREERS WORKING WITH CHILDREN

The teaching profession is the largest in the world, and certainly one of the most important, for teachers have the responsibility of transmitting knowledge from one generation to the next. This task has become even more difficult in recent years with the explosion of knowledge that has occurred. Although teaching jobs are available at levels from preschool to college to continuing education programs for adults, this chapter will focus on teaching jobs involving the education of children. Today, a person who teaches children may teach a special subject such as art, music, or physical education or instruct gifted and handicapped children.

ATTRIBUTES OF A TEACHER

Not everyone has the personality to be a teacher. Some teachers make learning come alive and inspire the children in their classes, while others produce monotonous lessons that bore their students. A successful teacher of children will have the following attributes:

- Enjoys being with children

- Is patient with children

- Keeps cool in trying situations involving children

- Gets satisfaction from helping children

- Has a pleasant-sounding voice

- Has a high energy level

- Is able to adapt to a new situation quickly

- Is able to control a group of children easily

- Is imaginative and creative

- Enjoys reading children's literature

- Enjoys playing with children

- Enjoys spontaneous activities

- Enjoys planning activities for children

- Is enthusiastic

- Is a self-starter

- Has a bit of a flair for acting

- Is open-minded

- Is organized

Anyone wanting to teach children should have most of these attributes in order to be well suited to this career.

PRESCHOOL TEACHERS

Children enter preschool, or nursery school, as it is often called, when they are 3 or 4 years old. They have no idea of what school is like except possibly from playing school with older brothers and sisters or neighborhood children. Preschool teachers have the task of introducing young children to school and preparing them for kindergarten. This doesn't mean teaching them to read or write or do workbook activities. Instead, it means helping children learn to get along in a classroom situation. They must be taught to listen attentively, to solve problems, to manipulate their hands effectively, to socialize with their classmates, to express themselves clearly, and to take care of their basic needs. Simultaneously, the preschool teacher must fan their desire to learn through interesting activities for groups and individuals. Good preschool teachers give young children a big boost up the school ladder of success. It is an excellent career consideration for prospective teachers who especially like young children.

Preparation for Becoming a Preschool Teacher

Employment requirements vary widely for preschool teachers. Most states require teachers to have a certificate to teach in a public preschool. These teachers usually have a four-year college degree in child development or early childhood education plus the necessary licenses. Preschool teachers at private schools usually face less stringent requirements. They may hold an associate's degree in early childhood education, as discussed in Chapter 2. Some enter the field through the Child Development Associate (CDA) program offered by the Council for Early Childhood Professional Recognition, also discussed in Chapter 2. In addition, preschool teachers can get training through the American Montessori Society, which offers many different programs.

What Being a Preschool Teacher Is Like

Long before the first child ever enters the classroom, preschool teachers have made preparations for the day. Lesson plans have been created describing what the children will do, storybooks have been selected, paints have been mixed, and craft projects have been set up. From the minute children walk through the classroom door, the teacher is busy greeting, guiding, assisting, and encouraging each individual student as well as organizing group activities. The teacher also has to spot children who are not feeling well, listen to complaints, and comfort the sad or injured child. Preschool teachers need to have an excellent understanding of children, how they develop, and their abilities at each age level. It is also essential that preschool teachers be capable of creating age-appropriate activities.

The Rewards of Teaching Preschool

Being a preschool teacher is immensely rewarding because these children really show affection for their teachers. Preschool teachers have the exceptional opportunity to fuel their students' energy and enthusiasm for future learning. The ability to start children off successfully on the educational path is satisfying.

Salary and Fringe Benefits

Preschool teachers' salaries are typically based on their education level and the number of years of teaching experience they have. At private schools, the rate of pay is often only an hourly wage. In general, the pay for preschool teachers is fairly low. In the 1990s, their median hourly wages were less than $10 an hour. However, preschool teachers working in public schools will typically earn higher wages, and those with state teacher certification generally have salaries and benefits comparable to kindergarten and elementary school teachers.

Benefits for preschool teachers, such as health insurance and paid vacations, vary widely, with some private schools providing good benefits and others offering no benefits. Teachers at this level, however, work relatively short hours. There is also the added bonus of having time off for all major holidays plus a long summer vacation.

The Personal Story of a Preschool Teacher

Cathy Johnson followed in the family tradition of teaching. Her mother taught at the first-grade level for 49 years. As she was growing up, Cathy observed her mother's love for teaching and saw the contribution to children's lives that her mother was making. To pursue her desired career as a preschool teacher, Cathy obtained a kindergarten endorsement and a master's degree in early childhood education.

Today, Cathy is a lead teacher in a preschool. She is responsible for selecting what will be taught in the classroom, planning how it will be taught, and teaching the lesson. In addition, Cathy has two aides who provide her with support in the classroom. Besides teaching, Cathy regularly holds conferences with parents and writes notes letting them know how their children are doing. Lead teachers also must handle the paperwork involved in running a class.

Cathy feels that a good preschool teacher must be patient and firm with his or her young students. At the same time, she says, it is necessary to be loving and very flexible. Cathy loves her job and says there are far more things she likes about it than she dislikes. Here are a few things Cathy likes about her job:

- It is never boring because there is so much variety.

- Each day at work is fun.

- She enjoys meeting the children's families and getting to know them well as she works closely with them.

- She has the opportunity to be creative throughout the work day.

- She likes working closely with her two aides, who help her keep the classroom running smoothly.

- The children constantly make her feel good because they genuinely like her.

- She does not have to spend much time keeping records, attending meetings, or writing reports.

- The shorter teaching hours give her more time to devote to her family.

- The school is very well equipped with brand-new playground equipment.

- She likes the openness and spontaneity of young children; she never knows what they will say or do.

Cathy's short list of dislikes is typical of many preschool teachers:

- She has inadequate benefits. The teachers at her preschool do not have health or medical insurance.

- The close-knit relationships that she forms with her preschool children vanish over the years. Five or ten years later, many do not remember Cathy when they see her on the street.

- The job is physically demanding; she must be able to bounce and jump around with the children.

- She tends to pick up ailments because so many children come to school sick.

Future

The demand for preschool teachers is increasing. More and more young children are now attending school earlier and earlier because both parents are working. In addition, the attention being focused on the problem of poor compensation for teachers is resulting in slightly higher wages and improved benefits.

KINDERGARTEN TEACHERS

Kindergarten and elementary school teachers play a vital role in the development of children. What is learned and experienced during the early years can shape children's views of themselves and the world and affect later success or failure in school, work, and life. Kindergarten teachers introduce young children to the world of letters and numbers, open their eyes to the joys of art and music, and help them learn about themselves and the world around them. They are challenged each day to provide interesting, exciting, and motivating ideas that will make young children want to learn. It has been said that all the important things that people need to learn in life are taught in kindergarten. These teachers show children how to share, respect others, tell the truth, and try to do their best at all times. Kindergarten teachers are more than teachers, they are also nurses, referees for fights, supervisors on the playground, temporary mothers or fathers, and, most importantly, friends to the children. They also happen to be giants in a world of miniature tables, chairs, easels, and playthings.

Preparation for Becoming a Kindergarten Teacher

Kindergarten teachers are considered elementary school teachers and will need to meet the same general requirements in order to teach at this level. The exact requirements for becoming an elementary school teacher vary from state to state. Today, all states and the District of Columbia require public school teachers to be certified. Generally, teachers must have a bachelor's degree and have completed an approved teacher training program with a prescribed number of education credits. Some five-year programs exist, and these generally lead to a master's degree as well as teacher certification. Traditional teacher education programs for kindergarten and elementary school teachers include courses designed specifically for those preparing to teach in reading, mathematics, science, social science, music, art, and literature. Prospective teachers must also take professional education courses prescribed by the state, such as philosophy of education, psychology of learning, and teaching methods. Teaching skills are acquired through supervised practice teaching in kindergarten or elementary school for about one semester. Because most school districts have continuing education requirements, teachers usually work toward master's degrees.

Many states have reciprocity agreements that make it easier for teachers who are certified in one state to become certified in another. In addition, there are emergency certificates for individuals who do not meet all requirements for a certificate when school districts cannot find enough certified personnel to employ.

Also, in most states, elementary teachers will have to pass a competency test demonstrating that they have certain basic skills in order to be licensed. One frequently used test is the National Teacher Examinations (NTE). This test is designed for college graduates majoring in education and consists of a core test and specialty area tests. Many states require teachers to get a minimum score on this test in order to obtain a teaching credential. Passing this test is a form of professional certification similar to that which accountants receive for passing the certified public accountant examination. School districts may require additional testing besides the NTE before teachers can enter the classroom.

What Being a Kindergarten Teacher Is Like

In the past, kindergarten classes were typically half-day classes with morning or afternoon sessions. Today, 40 percent of all kindergartens are full-day programs, and teachers typically teach all day. In the first semester of the school year, kindergarten lessons are similar to those taught in preschool, since many of the children have not attended school previously. More focus, however, will be placed on skills that the children will need in first grade. Then, in the second semester, kindergarten teachers seriously begin prereading activities, teaching the children the letters of the alphabet and the corresponding sounds. The children prepare for future math instruction by learning shapes and matching, sorting, and counting objects.

The Personal Story of a Kindergarten Teacher

Jackie McVey teaches kindergarten at a private cooperative kindergarten. The parents of her students take turns acting as aides in the classroom, which gives her help from two aides at all times. Not only does she have the opportunity to meet her students' parents, but many of their grandparents also often assist her. A cooperative school is really a family school. Families act as resource people and suggest interesting activities for the class.

As a kindergarten teacher, Jackie is the recipient of a continual flow of affection from the children. She points out that a kindergarten teacher needs to like not only working with children but also dealing with parents. The relationship between parents and teachers at this level is very important in helping young children do well in school.

ELEMENTARY SCHOOL TEACHERS

Teachers at this level usually don't have to handle many of the children's personal needs, unlike both preschool and kindergarten teachers. They are concerned with introducing children to academics as well as guiding the children's emotional, social, physical, and mental development. In the primary grades, one through three, emphasis is on the traditional three Rs. As the children proceed through elementary school, they also are taught history, science, health, and English.

What Being an Elementary School Teacher Is Like

Elementary school teachers spend most of their time in a classroom with a class ranging in size from 15 to 30 children. The school may have special teachers who will take their students for music, art, physical education, and library. Teachers can use this time for preparing lessons or grading papers. Although most elementary school teachers instruct one class of children in several subjects, in some schools two or more teachers teach as a team and are jointly responsible for a group of students in at least one subject. A small but growing number of teachers instruct multilevel classrooms, which have students at several different learning levels. Elementary school teachers are also expected to supervise their class on the playground and may have additional duties supervising lunchrooms, halls, and bus loading and unloading. Including activities outside of the classroom, many teachers work more than 40 hours per week.

Elementary school teachers plan lessons, prepare tests, grade papers, make out report cards, meet with parents, and attend faculty meetings and conferences. They also assign lessons, give tests, hear oral presentations, and oversee special projects. Teachers also have the job of keeping order in their classrooms and diagnosing and correcting learning problems.

Elementary school teachers are required to fill many roles:

- *Disciplinarian*—making sure that the children follow the set rules

- *Team player*—working with the other teachers and staff members in your school building

- *Communications expert*—expressing orally and in writing to parents and other educators how well the children in your class are performing

- *Listener*—hearing what the children in your class are saying about their problems

- *Referee*—solving problems that occur between students

- *Motivator*—encouraging students to want to acquire knowledge

- *Performer*—grabbing and keeping the attention of your class as you teach each lesson throughout the day

- *Secretary*—keeping records, filling out forms, and completing reports

- *Jack-of-all-trades*—having to teach music, art, physical education, and other subjects beyond the basics of your class

- *Lunchroom or playground monitor*—making sure that everyone is orderly

The Rewards of Being an Elementary School Teacher

Being an elementary school teacher is a good career choice for those who love being around children all day. They will see how their lessons are motivating young children to learn. They will delight in observing how the students in their classrooms are developing and learning during the year they spend with them.

Elementary school teachers can take pride in being active participants in teaching children the basic skills they will need throughout their lives.

The Personal Story of an Elementary School Teacher

Susan Lawton is a second-grade teacher in a large public school system. She got an early start in her profession because she worked in a school laboratory at a nursery school during college. Susan feels that her happiest moments in teaching come when her students from previous years return and tell her how they enjoyed her class. She finds it fascinating to see what they have done with their lives and what careers they have chosen. And it is satisfying to Susan to know that she can take credit for some of her former students' success.

Susan especially likes the start of each school year, when she gets to see former students and meet new children. The first day of school in her lesson plan books looks like this:

LESSON PLAN FOR SUSAN LAWTON
Grade: 2nd

9:20 1st Bell! Students enter and find own desk and chair. Encourage them to become acquainted with school materials on desks (folder, pencils, crayons, etc.). Morning Work: answer student questionnaire on favorite things.

9:30 2nd Bell! Opening Activities: take attendance, collect lunch money and parent notes, say pledge. Discuss how to listen to announcements each morning.

9:45 "Get acquainted" at big circle:
1. Discuss teacher bulletin board displaying teacher's favorite things.
2. Introduce the "Star Student" bulletin board.
3. Have children talk about summer vacations.

10:00 Children are to do summer vacation drawing project at their desks.

10:30 Discussion of classroom rules:
1. Proper handling of classroom objects.
2. Use of rest room passes.
3. Consequences for breaking rules.

11:00 Tour school building:
1. Show special classrooms (art, music, gym, library, computer room), cafeteria, school office, teacher's mailbox.
2. Introduce principal and secretary.

11:30 Class discussion:
1. Discuss homework policy.
2. Suggest study habits for home.
3. Recommend homework kit including markers, ruler, paper, pencils, etc.; also, recommend keeping a box for storing each grading period's work.
4. Explain grading system.
5. Give tips on how to be successful in second grade.

12:00 Discuss lunch and recess procedures.

12:15 Lunch and 12:45 recess.

1:20 Rest room break.

1:30 Story time.

1:45 Me Project: construct personalized cubes using magazines to find pictures of favorite items, hobbies, sports, etc., to glue on cubes. (Pass out glue, scissors, cubes.)

2:30 Distribute textbooks and show class how to organize them in desks with morning books on the left, afternoon books on the right.

3:00   Go over how papers are to be headed. Pass out lined paper. Practice writing first and last names, teacher's name, and school. Write sentences together about first day of school.

3:30   Free play: allow children time to familiarize themselves with classroom games and socialize with new and old school friends.

3:50   Discuss cleaning-up procedures and then clean up.

3:55   Discuss dismissal procedures and listen quietly for day-end announcements.

4:00   Announcements.

4:05   1st Bell! Bus students leave with patrol person.

4:10   2nd Bell! Walkers and riders follow patrol person. Prepare next day's morning work (school word search). Put stickers on incentive charts for those who earned them.

4:20   Pull shades and close door.

JUNIOR HIGH OR MIDDLE SCHOOL TEACHERS

Junior high and middle school teachers work with children as they are starting to cross the bridge from childhood to adolescence. Rather than teach a wide variety of subjects, these teachers concentrate on teaching within a single subject area such as mathematics, English, science, social studies, reading, art, music, and physical education. Junior high and middle school teachers may hold either general elementary or secondary credentials. Preparation for teaching at this level will vary. In general, coursework will include education courses dealing with psychology, tests and measurements, methods of teaching in the special subject area, and student teaching in that area. In addition, college courses in the subject area will give prospective teachers a solid knowledge of the subject they teach.

Teachers at this grade level can climb the career ladder to become department heads. In this position they are responsible for all the teachers teaching the same general subject, such as English, mathematics, or science. They teach some classes and help the other teachers in the department decide what is to be taught in each class, as well as help them with any problems. At many schools they are also involved in rating teacher performance.

What Being a Junior High or Middle School Teacher Is Like

Being a junior high or middle school teacher is like being both an elementary school and a senior high school teacher. The children receive more guidance than high school students but at the same time have separate teachers for each subject. Teachers at this level will teach five or more classes in their subject area and have a free period during the day to devote to preparation. For each class, they will write lesson plans, make and correct tests, collect homework, and contact parents when necessary. They will be required to perform routine bookkeeping tasks like taking attendance for every class and keeping track of issued textbooks. Besides classroom-oriented work, many junior high and middle school teachers are involved in supervising extracurricular activities.

The Rewards of Teaching Junior High or Middle School

It is a pleasure for junior high and middle school teachers to concentrate their teaching efforts on a subject where they have considerable expertise and interest. Furthermore, they have the opportunity to see the children in their classes mature during the school year and to play an important part in helping them grow up.

The Personal Story of a Middle School Teacher

Titus Exum teaches eighth-grade American history. He has a bachelor's degree in elementary education and a master's in school administration and supervision. He holds elementary credentials in Missouri and Alaska. To obtain his present job, Titus had to take the National Teacher Examinations.

Titus works as part of a five-person teaching team. Each teacher teaches only one subject; however, they work together to plan assemblies, select guest speakers, arrange field trips, organize field days, and handle other situations involving all of the eighth-grade teachers. He finds that the hardest part of his job is motivating students who are not interested in learning history.

ELEMENTARY TEACHERS OF SPECIFIC SUBJECTS

Some teachers concentrate on teaching children a specific subject in elementary school. For example, many elementary schools have reading teachers, music teachers, art teachers, and physical education teachers on their staffs. These teachers are generally required to have bachelor's degrees in education with special training in their subject area. They will typically hold elementary school credentials with an endorsement in their special area.

The Personal Story of an Elementary School Music Teacher

Teaching music is an excellent way to share a love of music with children. Music teachers do have to make lesson plans, take attendance, and give grades, just like other elementary school teachers. Their work is not easy, as they may see over 500 students in a week. In addition, state or district guidelines frequently prescribe the curriculum that is to be taught in music classes. Besides normal teaching duties, most music teachers will usually spend time before and after school working with different musical groups and preparing students for special contests and performances.

Julia Scherer has taught music at the same elementary school for more than 20 years. She graduated from college with a bachelor's degree in music education. Like most music teachers, Julia has obtained a master's degree in music and taken additional courses. As an elementary music specialist, Julia teaches general music classes, which feature instruction in vocal music, composers, music reading, instruments of the orchestra, music appreciation, and playing the recorder.

SPECIAL EDUCATION TEACHERS

Special education teachers work with the learning disabled, the visually and hearing impaired, and those with mental and physical disabilities. In this job, they work closely with doctors, social workers, psychologists, speech pathologists, occupational and physical therapists, and parents to make sure that each child's individual learning plan is helping the child learn to the best of his or her ability. Special education teachers do not always work in a classroom. They may work at clinics, in resource rooms in schools, or in residential centers. The demand for teachers in this area is very high.

In areas where many children are immigrants and do not have adequate English language skills, teachers are hired as ESL (English as a Second Language) teachers. Their job is to help these children catch up with their classmates. With immigration to the United States increasing, demand for teachers in this area is expected to remain high. Special certification is required to be an ESL teacher.

The Personal Story of a Special Education Teacher

Lysandra Walker is a teacher of the deaf. Deafness is the hardest sensory loss to overcome, as people learn so much through hearing what others say. Lysandra spends her days bridging the communication gap between her students and teachers and administrators. She interprets for assemblies and classes. She also helps educate the teachers and administrators on the educational needs of the deaf. And above all else, she teaches communications skills to all her students.

SALARY AND FRINGE BENEFITS

The salaries of teachers in public schools are based on the degrees they hold and the number of years they have taught. The average salary for public elementary school teachers in 1998–1999 was about $40,582 a year according to the National Education Association. The highest average salary was $51,584, in Connecticut, and the lowest was $28,552, in South Dakota. Earnings in private schools were generally lower. Many teachers work during the summer in the school system or in other jobs, often education related.

Public school teachers have benefits packages that typically include health insurance and life insurance. Furthermore, they have paid sick leave, and most school districts also allow leave days for conducting personal business, handling family emergencies, and jury duty. On certain days during the school year, teachers meet with parents or attend in-service training sessions instead of teaching in the classroom. Teachers frequently join unions, such as the American Federation of Teachers and the National Education Association. These unions bargain with school systems over wages, hours, and the terms and conditions of employment, which may include such issues as class size and pay for supervising extracurricular activities.

Most public school teachers are obliged to participate in a retirement program under either a state teachers' retirement system or a state public employees' retirement system. Both teacher and school district contribute to retirement programs. Some of these programs offer good retirement benefits. Unfortunately, these benefits cannot be transferred from state to state.

SPECIAL BENEFITS

Certain benefits are unique to the teaching profession. The work year is typically 180 days long. This includes a long summer break (about two months) plus a two-week break in December and one-week break in the spring. Some school districts now have one-week winter breaks in January. In a number of school districts, teachers now work in year-round schools with breaks between each session and a longer break during the year.

Teachers who have been employed in a school district for a specific number of years and have done their job in a satisfactory manner receive tenure. Tenure is not a guarantee of a job, but it does provide some security. Tenured teachers cannot be fired without just cause and due process. Tenure is usually granted after a probationary period, typically three years.

FUTURE

A national teacher shortage is on the horizon, according to the National Education Association. The number of elementary school job openings will increase substantially as a large number of teachers retire and student enrollment increases. How many teachers will actually be employed depends on state and local expenditures for education. Pressure from taxpayers to reduce expenditures could result in fewer teachers being hired, while pressure to improve the quality of education could result in more.

EARLY PREPARATION FOR A TEACHING CAREER

The best way to prepare for a teaching career is by working with children, either as a paid employee or as a volunteer. Working with children as a baby-sitter is an excellent way to start learning how to deal effectively with children. Jobs in summer camps or at child care centers also give valuable experience, as does volunteer work with youth organizations such as the Boy and Girl Scouts and YMCA groups. Teaching as a career can be explored through teaching at a Sunday school or working as a tutor. In high school, there are cadet teaching programs for those interested in a teaching career.

OTHER JOBS IN THE EDUCATION ARENA

The focus of this chapter is on classroom teaching. Some teachers will want to climb the career ladder and become curriculum directors, assistant principals, principals, assistant superintendents, and superintendents. In these jobs, they will still be working for the welfare of children but will no longer be directly involved with their students.

At every school, jobs other than teaching let individuals work closely with children:

School counselor. Elementary school counselors are involved mostly in social and personal counseling. They work with children individually, in small groups, or with entire classes. These counselors also consult and work with parents, teachers, school administrators, school psychologists, school nurses, and social workers. Most school counselors work the traditional nine- to ten-month school year and generally have the same hours as teachers. All states require school counselors to hold state school counseling certification. Some states also require public school counselors to have both counseling and teaching certificates. Depending on the state, a counselor may need two to five years of teaching experience plus a master's degree in counseling in order to get a counseling certificate.

School nurse. Elementary schools may employ school nurses, or one nurse may meet the needs of several schools. School nurses provide a variety of services to students, including giving first-aid treatment for injury and symptoms of illnesses, checking immunization records, performing health screening tests, updating medical records, and teaching in health classes. All school nurses are registered nurses. Some states require the completion of certain education courses and/or a teacher credential to hold this job.

School secretary. This job involves handling all of the secretarial duties of a school. This will include recording attendance and maintaining students' records. Because the setting for this work is a school, the secretary will also spend time dealing with children's questions and helping with ill and injured children.

School bus driver. Twice a day, school bus drivers in their big yellow buses are working with children. In the morning, they pick the children up at scheduled stops; in the afternoon they return the children home. In addition, they may drive the children on field trips or provide transportation to other schools for special services. Bus drivers must possess the appropriate state driver's licenses.

Tutor. Tutors provide children with special help in one or more subject areas. They may work in their own homes or go to the children's homes after school, in the evening, or on weekends. Tutors typically charge an hourly rate.

APPLYING FOR A JOB IN THE EDUCATION ARENA

Chapter 12 discusses the details of applying for a job. One step involved in obtaining a job is completing an application. The application shown in Figure 6.1 shows the type of information job seekers must supply to school systems.

Figure 6.1   Application for Teaching Position

Date_____

ASSIGNMENT PREFERENCE (1)_____ (2)_____
(Subject or Grade Level)

AREA(S) OF
CERTIFICATION_____
                                    Major   Minor

        Bachelor's Degree: Major:_____ Minor:_____
                                           Semester or Quarter Hours

        Master's Degree: Major:_____ Minor:_____
                                           Semester or Quarter Hours

        Graduate hours completed
        beyond Bachelor's or Master's Degree
                        Bachelor_____ Master_____

NAME _____
            Last   First   Middle/Maiden

Present Address_____
                                                    Street

_____ Telephone_____
            City   State   Zip   (include area code)

Permanent Address_____
                                                    Street

_____ Telephone_____
            City   State   Zip   (include area code)

Date of Birth_____ Place of Birth_____
                        (optional)   (optional)

Social Security No._____ Teacher Retirement No._____
                                                            (if applicable)

I EDUCATIONAL DATA

List the high school, colleges, and universities attended or graduated.

	Name of Institution	Location	Dates of Attendance	Degree	Subjects Major/Minor
High School					
College (or) University					
Graduate					
Other					

I am a candidate for the _____ degree to be conferred about _____.

II LICENSE DATA

Applicants should possess a valid teaching certificate or be taking necessary steps to obtain such certification.

Applicant has taken and passed all necessary tests to qualify for certification by the Department of Education.   Yes_____   No_____

Type License	Number	Expiration Date	Subjects or Grades

III REFERENCES

May we have permission to secure your credentials?   Yes_____   No_____

Bureau or Agency_____

Address_____

Please list three references, including present and former principals, department heads, or college instructors under whom you have worked. Serious consideration of your application may necessitate communication with one or more of these references. Please indicate a date after which we might make such an inquiry.

Name	Position	Present Address	Telephone Number

IV EXPERIENCE DATA

Total number of contracted years teaching and/or administrative experience _____,
subject to verification. Must meet criteria set forth in Article IX (Teaching Experience Credit) of
current teacher contract.

School & Location	Dates From To	# of Contract Days per Year	Subject or Grades	Reason for Leaving

STUDENT TEACHING: (if completed within last three years)

School & Location	Dates From To	Subject or Grades	Supervising Teacher's Name and Address

WORK EXPERIENCE OTHER THAN TEACHING: (include military)

Employer & Location	Dates From To	Position or Rank	Reason for Leaving

Coaching Experience of _____

VARSITY COACHING (List in consecutive order beginning with most recent.)

Sport	Girls	Boys	Date From To	Record Won Lost	School District

OTHER COACHING (List in consecutive order beginning with most recent.)

Sport	Girls	Boys	Date From To	Record Won Lost	School District

Additional Information

List extracurricular activities in which YOU participate—check if willing to direct.

Activities	High School	College	Willing to Direct	Activities	High School	College	Willing to Direct

List positions of responsibility and leadership that YOU have held.

Positions	High School	College	Positions	High School	College

List any special honors YOU have received.

High School	College

Do you play a musical instrument(s)? Yes_____   No_____

Instrument _____ Years Played ____ Instrument _____ Years Played ____

V ADDITIONAL DATA

We are interested in any further information about you that may distinguish your application. This might include travel, honors, publications, advanced study, participation in special programs, extracurricular activities, civic and/or special interests.

_____

_____

_____

_____

_____

_____

_____

_____

_____

Are you now under contract?_____
When are you available for an interview?_____

The information submitted on this application is accurate to the best of my knowledge. I understand that my application will be retained in current files for a period of one year.

_____   _____

　　　　Signature of Applicant　　　　　　　　　　　　　　Date

•••

PROCESSING OF APPLICATION (For Office Use Only)

Interviewed by:_____ Date_____

_____

_____

_____

Grade and Step _____

Salary_____

School Assignment_____

REQUEST FOR BACKGROUND INFORMATION

To All Applicants:

The job for which you are applying with the _____ SCHOOL involves contact with our student population. Please complete the questions below to help us evaluate your suitability to work with these students. All applicants for employment are expected to provide us with this information; you are not being singled out for closer inspection. This insert is part of the Application itself and any misrepresentation or omission of fact may be grounds for disqualification from further consideration or for termination from employment regardless of when the misrepresentation or omission is discovered.

Are you presently the subject of any investigation or other procedure which considers or could lead to your discharge for misconduct by your present employer? Yes ___ No ___. If yes, explain the circumstances on a separate sheet and attach it to this application.

Have you ever resigned from a prior position, similar to the one for which you are applying, under circumstances involving your employer's investigation of your sexual contact with another person, mishandling of funds, or criminal conduct? Yes ___ No ___. If yes, explain the circumstances on a separate sheet and attach it to this application.

*Have you ever been the subject of a charge or investigation by your current or prior employer(s) or a law enforcement agency, implicating you in the sexual abuse of another person? Yes ___ No ___.

*Have you ever pleaded guilty or "no contest" (nolo contendere) to, or been convicted of, any criminal offense? Yes ___ No ___.

If you have answered yes to either of the previous two questions*, please explain, in detail, including the date of the charge, the court action, the offense in question, and the address of the court involved (attach additional pages if necessary):

_____

_____

_____

Conviction of a crime is not an automatic bar to employment. _____ SCHOOL will consider the nature of the offense, the date of the offense, and the relationship between the offense and the position for which you are applying.

AUTHORIZATION AND RELEASE

My signature below constitutes authorization to investigate and examine my employment history and evaluations, as well as my criminal record (if any), in the custody of any private or public employer or any state, local, or federal agency. I further authorize those persons, agencies, or entities that the _____SCHOOL contacts in connection with my employment application to fully provide the _____SCHOOL any information on the matters set forth above. I expressly waive in connection with any request for or provision of such information any claims, including without limitation defamation, emotional distress, invasion of privacy, or interference with contractual relations, that I might otherwise have against the _____ SCHOOL, its agents and officials, or against any provider of such information.

I HAVE READ THIS AUTHORIZATION AND RELEASE OF ALL CLAIMS, AND I EXPRESSLY AGREE TO THE TERMS SET OUT HEREIN.

_____   _____

SIGNATURE   DATE

_____

PLEASE PRINT YOUR NAME

THE CHALLENGE OF TEACHING

Teachers shape future generations. The more skilled they are, the more they can help children master the complexities of living in today's world. Teachers are constantly challenged to find new and innovative techniques to motivate each child to learn in his or her special way. They also are called on to handle a wide variety of supercharged emotions, from helping a young child adjust to being away from home for the first time to getting a hyperactive child to stay in his or her seat. They are working at a job that is rewarding, challenging, hectic, and never boring.

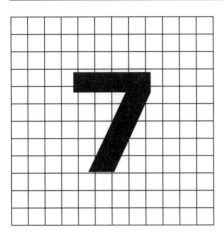

CHILDREN'S SPORTS AND RECREATION CAREERS

Many children spend much of their leisure time participating in a wide variety of organized sports and recreation activities. Interesting careers await those who wish to help children gain sports skills or enjoy their recreation time. These careers truly present an opportunity to combine avocation and vocation. Karate aficionados can spend their workdays introducing children to the intricacies of karate. Former basketball players can share their skills with children eager to follow in their footsteps. Camp counselors and directors can help children develop a love of the outdoors. YMCA/YWCA instructors can introduce children to new recreational pursuits. All of these careers let individuals share enjoyable activities with children.

CAREERS IN SPORTS ACTIVITIES

Combining a desire to work with children and sports can lead to career opportunities in almost any area of the country where there is a sufficient population of children. Sports are organized athletic activities played individually or in teams. Children are able to learn to play most sports. Few children will go on to earn their living playing a sport; however, sports bring children great enjoyment and satisfaction during their school years and can lead to a lifetime of interest and participation in sports activities. Through sports, children are able to learn many different skills, including ones not just related to sports, such as:

- Handling defeat and victory

- Being part of a team

- Making a contribution to a group effort

- Learning to follow rules

- Learning how to play fair

- Learning how to overcome adversity

- Disciplining their emotions

There are opportunities for careers teaching children such sports activities as swimming, gymnastics, tennis, golf, bowling, ice-skating, bicycling, basketball, baseball, horseback riding, archery, badminton, ice hockey, soccer, scuba diving, fishing, or fencing. Parents are willing to pay for both private and group instruction in sports to help their children gain skills that may lead to a professional career, participation in a sport while in school, or a lifetime of enjoyment.

THE SETTING

Individuals who want to instruct children in a particular sport work in a number of different settings where the sport can be taught and practiced.

Nonprofit youth associations provide competitive sports opportunities for children in football, baseball, softball, and soccer.

Private clubs offer classes at tennis, golf, swimming, and other facilities for children anxious to master a particular sport.

Parks departments frequently provide instruction in specific sports at facilities designed for those sports.

Commercial sports centers have the facilities for instruction in one sport, such as bowling, tennis, golf, swimming, or ice-skating.

Privately owned sports facilities are centers for instruction in such sports as karate, gymnastics, and boxing.

PREPARATION FOR BECOMING A SPORTS INSTRUCTOR

Individuals who are planning to become volunteer coaches can find out about the special training and certification requirements from the National Youth Sports Coaches Association (NYSCA), which is part of the National Alliance for Youth Sports. This organization has a nonprofit certification program that improves the quality and safety of out-of-school sports. Coaches learn first-aid safety, teaching techniques, the psychology of coaching, sports ethics, and how to make practice sessions interesting and fun.

Sports instructors need to have a thorough understanding of the sport they teach. This means knowing the rules of the sport, the techniques needed to gain skill in the sport, and how to teach the sport to children. Many sports have professional associations that offer training programs for instructors. For example, the United States Professional Tennis Association has programs and conferences throughout the year for tennis professionals. For swimming instructors, the American Red Cross has an instructional and certification program. Sports instructors also need to keep current in what is happening in their individual sports through reading magazines, books, and newsletters in their sports areas.

APTITUDES OF A SPORTS INSTRUCTOR

Besides knowing how to teach and having a genuine desire to work with children, sports instructors need to have the following aptitudes to be successful in their careers:

- Understanding of how each student learns the best
- Ability to communicate with children and their parents
- Ability to share their personal enthusiasm for a sport
- Ability to teach a sport to children with a wide range of abilities, from those who are destined to be champions to those who have limited talents
- Good sense of humor
- Ethics
- High moral standards
- Ability to treat all children fairly
- Ability to handle children's emotional outbursts
- Knowledge of how to build children's self-esteem
- Ability to help children develop confidence in their own abilities
- High energy level

WHAT BEING A SPORTS INSTRUCTOR IS LIKE

Sports instructors who concentrate on teaching sports skills and techniques to children generally work the hours that children are not in school. They may start work around 3:00 P.M. and work until 9:00 P.M. or even later. Most instructors also have a very full workday each Saturday. In the summer, they are able to concentrate their work in the daytime. However, in sports such as ice-skating and tennis, where limited time is available at facilities, instructors may need to begin work as early as 5:00 A.M. There are opportunities in this field for part-time as well as full-time positions.

Most sports instructors will give private lessons as well as work with groups. They have to keep track of the progress that each child and group is making and adjust their teaching programs to meet the children's needs. There is some record keeping involved in being a sports instructor, such as recording who attends each session. Unless sports instructors own a facility, they are not involved in the business side of sports instruction.

Being a sports instructor frequently involves more than teaching children a sport. When children enter competitions, sports instructors frequently accompany them to provide additional coaching. In many sports, instructors are responsible for setting up and running competitions and tournaments.

The Personal Story of a Tennis Professional

P. A. Nilhagen was an excellent junior tennis player. He gave his first tennis lesson in Sweden when he was only 16 and earned six Swedish crowns (about 75 cents). Today, he is the Director of Junior Development for one of the largest tennis programs in the United States.

P.A. was ranked in the top 10 of Sweden's junior division at the ages of 17 and 18. He was also a member of the Swedish Junior Davis Cup Team. P.A.'s tennis accomplishments led to a college scholarship in the United States. For four years, he played tennis at Western Kentucky University.

P.A. underwent special schooling and training in order to become a tennis pro. In Sweden, he took training courses to gain certifications. Once in the United States, P.A. became certified by the United States Professional Tennis Association (USPTA). At Western Kentucky University, he received a bachelor's degree in physical education. Today, P.A. continues his tennis education by regularly attending the USPTA's teachers conference held in New York City during the U.S. Open tennis tournament, as well as several other USPTA-sponsored conventions. He subscribes to eight tennis magazines and reads every available tennis book to learn more about the sport. Also, P.A. studies videotapes of televised tennis matches.

P.A.'s first job was as a tennis pro at a very large midwestern tennis facility. After only a few months, he became head pro and shortly thereafter director of the club's junior development program. P.A. is the only coach in the Midwest to remain at one club for more than 20 years. For the greater part of the year, he teaches in the club's indoor facilities. When summer comes, he is outdoors running one of the largest youth tennis programs in the nation.

P.A.'s daily schedule begins at about 5:00 A.M., when he gets up and eats a healthy breakfast. By 7:00 A.M., P.A. has arrived at work, one hour before the first scheduled lesson, to prepare for the day. From then until 5:00 P.M., P.A. is in charge of all on-court activities, which include group lessons, private instruction, and challenge matches. From 5:00 P.M. till 7:00 P.M., he spends time in parent or player meetings.

Even though it is late, P.A.'s day is not over yet. He will probably spend another hour or two talking on the phone with players, discussing strategies and approaching matches. As you can see, a tennis pro does not always work a 40-hour week.

P.A. believes a teacher must do his or her best with every student. He is motivated to find different things in each child's game so that lessons will never be boring for him or the student he is teaching. P.A. is never late for a lesson—he respects his students too much to be late. He sees himself doing the same job five years from now—only better because he will have had five more years of experience.

Some of P.A.'s happiest moments on the job are when his students win state, western, or national titles or compete professionally. He especially remembers being at Wimbledon with Todd Witsken and another time when his stepson won the state doubles championship.

P.A.'s advice to prospective teachers or coaches of any sport is to make sure that you love your sport and the people you will be training in that sport. He also suggests finding a role model whom you can emulate. Finally, P.A. believes that sports teachers should stay fit and dress professionally.

The Personal Story of the Owner of a Gymnastics Facility

Terry Spence was a member of the 1968 Olympic gymnastics team but had to leave the squad because of a sprained ankle. Then, while working out for the 1972 Olympic Games, she took a terrible fall. Everyone thought her back was broken. At that moment, Terry, not knowing if she would ever walk again, decided she would teach the sport she loved from a wheelchair if her competitive career was over. Fortunately, Terry's back was not broken, and she was able to end her career in a burst of glory at the 1973 World University Games in Moscow, where she competed against Olympic gold medalist Olga Korbut. At these games, Terry finished the highest, up to that time, for a female gymnast from the United States.

After Terry's competitive gymnastics career was over, she briefly promoted gymnastics for the owner of several gymnastics camps before opening her own studio. When Terry first started her studio, she worked from ten in the morning till one in the afternoon and then returned to the gym at four and stayed until ten at night. Soon, her World of Gymnastics studio had a staff of 13 and more than 500 students attending classes for fun and at 10 different team competition levels. The studio was open six days a week. On Sundays, the coaches took the students to meets or meets were hosted at her studio. Terry's efficient staff allowed her to trim her teaching hours to between 4:00 P.M. and 10:00 P.M. She was able to reserve the mornings for doing paperwork at home; other staff members taught the sessions for preschoolers.

Terry's happiest moments on the job came when her gymnastics team did well in competition, because she knew she had helped them reach this skill level. On the downside, she found it difficult to deal with parents who expected too much from their children, as well as those who did not believe their children had any potential. Nevertheless, she managed to deal with the parents because she cared so much about teaching children gymnastics.

Terry points out that owning a gym requires one special aptitude: stamina. Owners must have the strength to handle the staff, parents, children, and themselves, along with all the problems running a studio brings.

She feels that the most difficult thing about owning a studio is all the paperwork involved in operating a business, from collecting money and paying rent to buying insurance.

More Jobs

Individuals should not feel confined to careers in the more traditional sports. While most children have bicycles and enjoy riding them, some children race their bicycles on racing tracks and need instruction to learn more about this sport. Sports instructors teach children archery on indoor and outdoor ranges. Many children are also interested in the martial arts. Name a sport, whether it is scuba diving or snowboarding, and individuals can be found teaching children that sport.

CAREERS IN RECREATION

Recreation refreshes children's minds and bodies. There are some children, however, whose sole concept of recreation is watching television. But recreation is far more than passive watching. It involves playing games, participating in sports, enjoying hobbies, and relaxing. Professionals in the field of recreation introduce children to the vast number of ways they can use their leisure time enjoyably. Their workplace is in parks, playgrounds, gymnasiums, camps, hotels, and even aboard cruise ships and at dude ranches. They work for YMCA/YWCAs, scouting and youth organizations, fraternal organizations, neighborhood clubs, private clubs, tourist businesses, and camps. Most recreation specialists, however, are employed by city and county agencies and work in their park and recreation departments. While the demand for professionals in recreation is increasing, individuals interested in this career need to remember that the number of people employed in recreation is very small compared to those employed as child care workers or teachers.

Aptitudes of a Recreation Worker

Every professional must have certain aptitudes to be effective. Those who want to work with children in the field of recreation need to be far more than "playground baby-sitters." Some of the aptitudes that recreation professionals should have include the following:

- An ability to motivate children to take part in activities

- An understanding of how to teach skills to children

- An understanding of appropriate activities for children of different ages

- An ability to plan and organize activities

- A genuine love of recreational activities and the ability to transmit that love to children

- An understanding of the kinds of recreational activities children need to round out their lives

- An ability to work effectively with children of different ages

- An ability to work closely with others in developing and executing a program for children

Training

Volunteers were once the main source for recreation workers in communities. However, as more and more attention is focused on the recreational needs of both children and adults, competent professionals are required to administer, supervise, and run programs. To meet this need, many colleges have increased the number of courses offered in recreation. These courses are often part of the curriculum in the health, physical education, and recreation departments. An increasing number of full-time recreation professionals now have degrees from two- and four-year college programs. Besides courses in recreation, they take classes in psychology, sociology, communications, and the performing arts. Another important part of their education is on-the-job training in the field for college credit. Even more education is needed by those who want to hold administrative positions in very large recreation and park programs: they are often required to have a master's degree in recreation. While a degree in recreation is helpful in getting a job, it is not essential. Many individuals working in recreation have degrees in physical education, health, forestry, education, and even areas unrelated to recreation. Having work and volunteer experience during the high school or college years does help individuals find careers in recreation. It also helps to be able to teach a skill such as swimming, archery, or canoeing to children.

Recreation Jobs in Community Programs

During the summer most communities have children's outdoor recreation programs in parks. Throughout the year they will have indoor programs in multi-purpose centers. Recreation professionals are needed to administer programs at individual parks and centers as well as the entire program of a community. The title of "direct leader" is given to recreation professionals who work closely with children. They are the ones who organize sports contests, bike rodeos, and dramatic productions. They also teach children to swim, play tennis, or dance. Their job frequently includes supervising playground activities and running arts and crafts programs. Full-time leaders need degrees in recreation or related fields. College students can find part-time jobs as direct leaders during the summer and school year. Their salaries are hourly, while full-time leaders' pay is comparable to teachers' pay.

The Personal Story of a YMCA Leader

The entry-level position as a salaried professional at a YMCA/YWCA is as a program director. Program directors are college graduates. Their duties include creating and implementing recreation programs such as adult and youth aquatics, youth sports, parent/child programs, child care, camps, and youth leadership programs.

Thom Martin's career at the YMCA really began at the age of 8 months, when he made a big splash in the parent/infant swim program. Since then, the YMCA has been a constant presence in his life, from youth camping and swimming programs to beginning his career at the "Y." While attending high school, Thom served as a YMCA swim instructor, day-camp counselor, lifeguard, movement education instructor, and coach in youth sports. During college, he worked part time as a child care program leader and was also manager of the YMCA pool in the summer. After graduation from college, he became the program director at the YMCA where he worked during college. As program director, he handled camping, teen, and parent/child programs. While overseeing the Youth and Government program, he was recognized as Advisor of the Year.

Recognition of his skill as a program director led to Thom's becoming one of the youngest executive directors of a YMCA facility. As executive director, he is responsible for program development as well as regionwide camping programs. Thom explains that YMCA camp is far more than just a fun place for kids to spend time during the summer. He describes it as a place where they can learn and grow, under the guidance of caring counselors, in programs designed especially for them.

Thom says that a YMCA career gives young professionals far more responsibility far sooner than many management jobs. The most rewarding part of his job, however, is the positive impact that many YMCA programs have on children's lives.

What Being a Worker at Summer Camp Is Like

At summer camps, children canoe, swim, ride horseback, toast marshmallows, and build memories that can last a lifetime. And all the professionals who work at the camp, from counselor to director, play a role in helping children learn new skills, gain confidence in their own abilities, and pick up valuable lessons about life. The size of a camp determines the number of employees. The larger a camp is, the more employees it needs to handle the campers, administrative tasks, and other jobs such as cooking, health care, and maintenance. The program staff teaches skills to the children. The counselors supervise groups of children. Division heads oversee several counselors, and the director is responsible for every facet of the camp. Except for the director, all of the staff members are usually just employed for the summer.

Camp counselor.   The people who work directly with children at summer camps are the counselors. They share cabins with the children, comfort the homesick, encourage the inexperienced to try new activities, help shy children learn to socialize, teach skills, and generally have fun with the children. Most camps hire college students for counselor positions. They also prefer counselors to have had experience as campers or working with children. In addition, counselors should demonstrate that they have:

- Good judgment

- Initiative and creativity

- Emotional stability

- Good moral character

- Good health and physical stamina

- Good rapport with children

Division head.   While the counselors have the direct responsibility of working with the children, someone has to plan and schedule the children's activities, arrange the staff schedule, handle serious problems, and see that the activities are running smoothly. These tasks are handled by division heads, who may have assistants. Division heads are typically in charge of several counselors who are supervising children of a specific age group. Most division heads began as campers and then served as counselors before entering their present positions.

Camp director.   At most camps, the only full-time employee is the camp director. The camp director has the ultimate responsibility for every aspect of the functioning of the camp, from seeing that camp rules are enforced to paying all the bills. The director also performs some tasks not listed in the usual job description, such as repairing leaky showerheads, driving the camp bus, or teaching a special class in karate. The director works at the camp during the summer, and in some cases may direct weekend camping sessions throughout the year. When directors are not actively involved in directing camps, they work on organizing and publicizing the next year's program.

What Working for the Boy Scouts of America Is Like

The mission of the Boy Scouts of America is to serve others by helping to instill values in young people, by helping them to achieve their full potential, and, in other ways, by preparing them to make ethical choices over their lifetime. Unlike some other social service organizations, professionals in the Boy Scouts are promoted from within. A bachelor's degree is required to be considered for an entry-level professional position. While work experience is an asset, it is not a prerequisite to working for the Boy Scouts. Most professionals start as district executives, a position responsible for all the scouting activities in a designated geographical area. The district executive recruits, guides, trains, motivates, and inspires the volunteer leaders. The starting salary is around $28,500; district executives are also given a car. Future salary will vary, because the Scouts are a merit-pay organization.

After three years, the district executive can expect to be promoted to a larger district or to start supervising entry-level personnel. The next step, four or five years later, is to a field position managing district executives or to a support program in an area like finance, fund-raising, or directing programs. Through classes at the regional and national levels, professionals receive training that prepares them for advancement in the organization.

Great opportunities exist to have an impact on boys' lives, not only through working in the Scout organization but also through serving as a volunteer. Troop leaders work directly with boys and can have the satisfaction of being a part of the good this organization does for boys.

THE BENEFITS OF A CAREER IN SPORTS AND RECREATION

One of the best aspects of a career working with children in sports and recreation is simply the opportunity to participate in enjoyable activities with children. While children are not always enthusiastic about school and may not be eager to visit health care professionals, they are generally enthusiastic about sports and recreation activities. Sports instructors have the pleasure of teaching children a sport they truly like, while recreation specialists can enjoy helping children learn ways to use their leisure time.

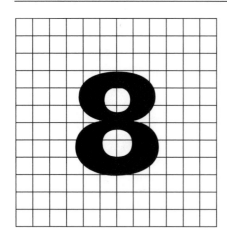

CHILDREN'S HEALTH CAREERS

Healthy children are happier and do better work in school. They are eager to play sports and take pleasure in hobbies and other recreational activities. They are better able to enjoy their families and friends. Because children's physical, mental, and social health is so important to their well-being, a great number of careers devoted to keeping children healthy have emerged. Although people tend to think of pediatricians when they think of a children's health career, many others work diligently to ensure that children remain healthy. There are pediatric specialists, nurses and nurse practitioners, pediatric dentists and their assistants, the staff of pediatrics wards and children's hospitals, and the psychiatrists, psychologists, and counselors who help ill or troubled children. A large number of compassionate individuals have chosen these careers because they want to help children, and the demand for these professionals continues to expand. They work in private practice, group practice, hospitals, and clinics.

THE HISTORY OF PEDIATRIC MEDICINE

Children's illnesses were mentioned in the literature of classical times, and a few books were written about the care of children during the medieval and early modern periods. Hospitals for the care of orphans have existed in Europe since one was built in Florence in 1421. The first hospital for children in the United States did not appear until shortly before the Civil War, when Dr. Abraham Jacobi established one in 1855 in New York City. It was not, however, until 1880 that a pediatrics section was organized within the American Medical Association and the medical profession recognized that children were not simply small adults. Children get diseases that adults rarely contract. Furthermore, children are continually growing, and disturbances in this process cause problems not seen in adults. In addition, the environment greatly affects the health of infants and children.

A great deal of knowledge about the treatment of children emerged in the twentieth century. Many serious diseases that were once considered fatal can now be treated successfully, so the emphasis in pediatrics has shifted toward prevention of illness. Furthermore, it is now recognized that each child has unique needs and special characteristics that must be considered in helping the child develop into a healthy adult.

As more and more knowledge about the health needs of children has been uncovered, a number of pediatric specialties have emerged. The number and variety of specialties is a boon for those who want to work with children in health care. Pediatric medical specialties include the following:

Adolescent medicine

Allergy/pulmonary

Audiology

Bronchopulmonary dysplasia

Cardiology

Cardiovascular surgery

Craniofacial anomalies

Counseling

Dentistry

Dermatology

Diabetes

Eating disorders

Endocrinology

Gastroenterology and nutrition

Genetic-metabolic

Genetics

Hand surgery

Hematology

Infant development

Infectious diseases

Neonatology

Neurogenetics

Neurology

Obesity

Oncology/bone marrow transplant

Ophthalmology

Orthopedics

Plastic surgery

Primary care

Psychiatry

Psychology

Renal

Research

Rheumatology

Speech-language pathology

Spina bifida

Surgery, general

Transplant, cardiopulmonary

Urology

THE EDUCATIONAL REQUIREMENTS OF HEALTH CARE PROFESSIONALS

Career possibilities within the medical field are wide open. Some training will be necessary for almost every career, with the exception of nursing aides, who receive employer training. There are vocational school and community college programs for those who wish to be technicians. For most careers as a health care professional, a college degree is required. Many careers require postgraduate education following college plus additional years of residency training. Furthermore, entry into postgraduate programs is very selective. Successful applicants demonstrate academic excellence and have high scores on graduate school admission tests.

THE DEMAND FOR MEDICAL PERSONNEL

Jobs are definitely available for those who want to work in areas related to children's health. The demand is fueled by the growing population of children and scientific discoveries and technological innovations that have created new treatments. There are even shortages of health care professionals in some areas. According to the American Hospital Association, 70 percent of hospitals are lacking qualified candidates for jobs.

PEDIATRICIANS AND PEDIATRIC NURSES

The professionals who concentrate on taking care of the basic health needs of children from birth to adult maturity are pediatricians and pediatric nurses. Besides special training, those choosing a career in this area must have the ability to work well with children and be able to deal effectively with their families. Of course, pediatricians and pediatric nurses are not the only medical professionals associated with the care of children. Physicians in general and family practice spend approximately one-fourth of their time caring for children. And nurses in hospitals, clinics, and offices also frequently handle the health needs of children.

What Being a Pediatrician Is Like

Today's pediatricians are more likely to work as salaried employees of group medical practices, clinics, or health care networks than in the past. Pediatricians in private practice may work 60 or more hours a week; however, pediatricians who work in groups have more time off because these organizations provide back-up coverage. While pediatricians spend the majority of their time seeing patients, considerable time is also devoted to dealing with parental concerns over the phone, making regular and emergency visits to hospitals, and keeping records.

The Personal Story of a Pediatrician

Caring for children is as rewarding as ever for Dr. Gustave (Stavie) Kreh, who has been in pediatric practice for more than 20 years. Stavie, who adores children, was attracted to pediatrics after working with children in summer camps during high school and college. After graduation from high school, Stavie attended Tulane University in New Orleans, where he majored in sociology and minored in history and chemistry while taking enough science courses to get into medical school.

Stavie attended the Louisiana State School of Medicine in New Orleans after graduating from college. Medical school, he says, teaches the facts and the how-to that every pediatrician needs, but he believes that his liberal arts degree is what gave him the foundation to be an excellent doctor. He wants students who are contemplating becoming doctors to realize that medical school is a tough grind even for students who did well in high school and college. Most medical students are overwhelmed by the tremendous amount of study and memorization that is required their freshman year. Stavie still remembers the first day of medical school, when he could not even pronounce the words on the professors' mimeographed handouts. Challenged by the difficulty and amount of work that was required of him, he battled back by studying eight to ten hours a day in class and then four or five more hours in the library at night.

"By the end of the intense, four-year medical program," Stavie points out, "you are like a sculpture. You have been chiseled, beaten, sat on, molded, melted down, and refined into a finished product." However, the sculpture was not yet finished: he then had to complete a three-year residency in pediatrics. When he recalls those years, Stavie remembers "horrendous hours, lousy pay, and twenty-four-hour duty every third day." At the same time, it was enjoyable because he was doing what he wanted to be doing.

After completing an army tour, Stavie joined a pediatric practice with four other doctors in Savannah, Georgia. Today, this practice has seven doctors and two nurse practitioners in what is one of the largest pediatric practices in the Southeast, with over 50,000 patients. Their office is open 365 days a year at 9:00 A.M. and stays open until every child has been seen, which could be as late as 8:00 P.M. in the winter or as early as 11:00 A.M. in the summer. On weekends and holidays only two doctors are in the office. Stavie designed the group's 10,000-square-foot office building, which has separate waiting rooms with different themes for well babies, sick children, adolescents, and new babies. The group also has two satellite offices.

A typical weekday for Stavie starts at 6:00 A.M., when he checks with his answering service for messages from patients and reports from partners. Then he is off to the two hospitals that the group services, where it usually takes him anywhere from one to two hours to visit his patients and confer with the nurses on each patient's progress or any potential medical problems. Around 9:00 A.M., Stavie arrives at the office, where he sees an average of 40 patients a day. On an extremely busy day, he may see up to 80 patients. While seeing so many patients may seem like assembly-line doctoring, Stavie says that most children have illnesses that are easily treated, including headaches, colds, and infections of the ears, respiratory system, and skin. When the occasional emergency arises, however, the pediatrician drops everything and goes to the hospital to take care of the child. Prospective pediatricians need to remember that besides treating sick children, they will also need to spend time attending conferences, monthly pediatric meetings, staff meetings, and hospital committee meetings. They must also oversee finances, computer operations, telephone systems, laboratory equipment, and hiring and scheduling staff.

To be a good pediatrician, Stavie feels, it is necessary to like children, work fast, tolerate night calls from scared parents, empathize with sick children, and have a sixth sense that helps you determine what is wrong when children cannot really tell you.

The happiest moments on the job for Stavie come when he is able to save a child from a life-threatening illness. He also loves when children drop by to see him before they go off to college, just to talk. Stavie's patients are like family to him, and he finds it very rewarding to see them grow physically and emotionally.

The Personal Story of a Pediatric Specialist

Pediatricians and family practitioners are the primary caregivers of children. However, they are aided in their work by specialists in the many pediatric health care fields mentioned earlier. Tom Southern, a plastic surgeon, is one of those specialists. During his junior year of medical school, he became totally hooked on a career as a plastic surgeon after seeing the difference a plastic surgeon could make in the life of a burned child. Today, 25 percent of his practice is devoted to the care of children.

A look at Tom's work schedule clearly shows that he is a very busy person. The most difficult part of his job is trying to get done everything that he wants done. Every Monday and Wednesday, Tom is in his office seeing patients continually from nine to five. However, his day does not begin at nine. Before office hours, he visits patients in two hospitals; after office hours, from 5:00 P.M. to 7:00 P.M., he will continue seeing hospital patients. On Tuesday, Thursday, and Friday, Tom is in surgery starting around 8:00 A.M. and continuing until 3:00 P.M. or sometimes 6:00 P.M. Three times a month he is on call in the hospital emergency room, and he also has to take his turn on call in his own private practice. Tom spends his days treating traumas and burns and doing reconstructive and cosmetic surgery. He has treated children as young as 1 month old.

What Tom likes most about plastic surgery is the variety of surgical procedures that he performs and the different personalities of his patients. However, he dislikes his lack of free time. His advice to anyone who is planning to enter the medical profession, especially plastic surgery, is to be prepared to immerse yourself in your job—but find time for yourself and your family.

Training for Pediatricians

All states require pediatricians, and all physicians, to be licensed. Licensing requirements include graduation from an accredited medical school (usually four years), completion of a licensing examination, and graduate medical education. Entry into a medical school requires three years of college or a bachelor's degree. Students spend the first two years of medical school primarily in laboratories and classrooms. They also learn to take case histories, perform examinations, and recognize symptoms. During the last two years, students work with patients under the supervision of experienced physicians. Following medical school, almost all doctors go directly on to graduate medical education, called a residency. Doctors seeking board certification in pediatrics take a final examination immediately after residency or after one or two years of practice. For those training in a subspecialty such as pediatric cardiology, even more years of residency are required.

What Being a Pediatric Nurse Is Like

Pediatric nurses are specially trained to provide nursing services to infants, children, and adolescents. They usually work in doctors' offices, hospitals, and clinics. They work closely with but subordinate to physicians in most cases.

To obtain a nursing license, all states require graduation from an accredited nursing school and passing a national licensing examination. Licenses must be periodically renewed, and continuing education is a requirement for renewal in most states.

Pediatric nurses perform most of the same duties as other nurses, except they work solely with children. They take temperatures and blood pressure and measure height and weight and record all this information in their young patients' medical folders. In the hospital, a pediatric nurse will be assigned to care for several children and will provide such services as taking the patients' vital signs, observing and recording their condition, and giving them medication—the same services adults require. A large part of a pediatric nurse's job is helping to reduce patients' anxiety about treatment.

Pediatric nurses need physical stamina because they spend considerable time walking and standing in their job. They need emotional stability to cope with the pain and suffering of children. Nursing has its hazards, especially in hospitals and clinics where pediatric nurses may care for children with infectious diseases such as hepatitis and AIDS (acquired immune deficiency syndrome). Nurses must observe rigid guidelines to guard against these and other dangers such as radiation, chemicals used for sterilization of instruments, and anesthetics. In addition, pediatric nurses face possible back injury when moving children, shocks from electrical equipment, and hazards posed by compressed gas.

The Personal Story of a Pediatric Nurse Practitioner

Dan Broekhuizen entered this profession because he loves working with children. He holds a bachelor's degree in nursing and a master's degree in nursing with a specialty in pediatrics. Most nurse practitioners hold master's degrees, although it is possible to do this work with a bachelor's degree plus additional training. Dan is employed in a pediatric clinic that has three pediatricians. A typical day at work for him involves seeing about 25 patients and handling well-baby appointments, physicals, and sick children. Between appointments, Dan has to make phone calls to answer questions from anxious parents about their children's health. According to Dan, pediatric nurse practitioners need physical examination and assessment skills plus the ability to discuss the medical needs of children in terms parents can understand. What he likes most about his job is dealing with children. The least favorite part of his job is dealing with parents.

Training for Nurses

There are three major educational paths to nursing:

1. *Associate's degree in nursing.* These programs are offered by community and junior colleges and take approximately two years to complete.

2. *Diploma.* Diploma programs are taught in hospitals and last two to three years. Very few nurses now graduate from these programs.

3. *Bachelor of Science in nursing.* These degrees are offered by colleges and universities and take from four to five years to complete.

Nursing education includes classroom instruction and supervised training in hospitals and other health facilities. Students take courses in anatomy, physiology, microbiology, chemistry, nutrition, psychology and other behavioral sciences, and nursing. Supervised clinical experience is provided in hospital departments such as pediatrics, psychiatry, and surgery.

Research is essential to find the right educational program in nursing at either the undergraduate or graduate level. Needs and interests must be considered, along with how well established the program's network of nursing contacts is, which will greatly assist the student in finding placement after graduation. The following questions should be asked about any nursing program:

1. Is the program accredited by the National League for Nursing? The National League for Nursing (NLN) of the American Nurses Association is the official professional accrediting body for programs in nursing. If a program is not accredited by the NLN, all coursework has to be evaluated before a nurse can continue in a higher nursing education program.

2. Upon graduating from the nursing program, will the school grant a degree in nursing? Many programs grant bachelor's degrees in fields other than nursing; however, graduating from one of these programs will pose

difficulties for graduates who are looking for admission to graduate nursing programs where a bachelor's degree in nursing is a prerequisite for admission.

3. What is the image and reputation of the school? Prospective nursing students should talk to graduates of the school and other nurses to find out more about a school as well as get additional information about the program from the National League for Nursing of the American Nurses Association.

4. What are the credentials of the faculty? Education lies in the hands of a school's faculty. Find out if faculty members are interested in research, have received awards for professional involvement or leadership in the field, and are active in professional organizations (and if so, which ones).

Salary and Fringe Benefits

Pediatricians are generally well paid, averaging over $130,000 a year in income after expenses. Those in pediatric specialties can expect higher incomes. The salary for registered nurses working full time ranges from less than $400 a week to approximately $900 a week. The median salary of nurse practitioners is about $70,000 a year.

Pediatricians in private practice will need to secure their own benefits. Pediatricians and pediatric nurses working in a group practice will participate in a group program. Pediatricians and pediatric nurses working at hospitals will have the benefits package offered at their workplace. In addition, nurses are often offered flexible work schedules, child care, educational benefits, bonuses, and other incentives.

CHILDREN'S DENTISTRY

Children need dental care to avoid certain dental problems as adults. The way gums and baby teeth are cared for affects the development of adult teeth. To ensure that their smiles remain perfect, young children go to pediatric dentists, pediatric hygienists, and orthodontists, as well as general practitioners of dentistry.

Demand

Although the demand for dentists is not expected to grow as fast as the average for all occupations through 2006, the demand for dental hygienists is expected to grow much faster than average. In the future, dentists are expected to hire even more hygienists to perform preventive dental care such as cleaning, so that they can use their own time for more profitable procedures such as surgery. Unless the number of hygienists increases sharply, opportunities for employment should remain very good in this medical profession.

What Being a Pediatric Dentist Is Like

While dentists may bring to mind images of drilling and filling cavities, dentists who work with children do their best to be seen as individuals who help children have bright healthy smiles. Many work in offices decorated to be appealing to children. They also strive to teach children how to care for their teeth through diet, brushing, flossing, the use of fluorides, and other aspects of dental care.

Although they do have to drill and fill cavities from time to time, pediatric dentists also examine x-rays, place protective plastic sealants on children's teeth, pull teeth, straighten teeth, and repair fractured teeth. They administer anesthetics and write prescriptions for antibiotics. In their work they use a variety of equipment, including x-ray machines, drills, and hand tools such as mouth mirrors, brushes, and scalpels.

The Personal Story of a Pediatric Dentist

In dental school, Donald Bozic found that he was attracted to pediatric dentistry because he was able to communicate well with children and enjoyed treating them. As soon as he graduated from dental school and was licensed to practice dentistry, he started his practice in pediatric dentistry. His training included:

- 4 years of college (B.S. in chemistry)
- 4 years of dental school
- 2 years of specialty training (residency in a hospital for children)

Without his specialty training, Donald could not have limited his practice to children's dentistry.

A typical day begins at 8:00 A.M. and finishes at approximately 5:00 P.M. Donald takes about one hour for lunch. His patients range from very young children to college students. No two patients are alike—not even twins! According to Donald, you need some special skills to be a good pediatric dentist:

- Exceptional patience
- Ability to listen
- Ability to practice excellent dental skills
- Ability to work quickly
- Acceptance that you are working with children

His work environment is definitely child-friendly. It is an open, airy office with a special "monkey room" where hundreds of stuffed toy monkeys cling to the wall. Each young patient can select one of the monkeys to hold while his or her teeth are treated. Donald's happiest moments on the job come when he is able to give children a positive attitude toward dentistry.

Salary and Fringe Benefits

In 1995, the net median income of dentists in private practice was about $120,000 a year, according to the American Dental Association. Dentists in specialty practices earned as much as $175,000. Many dentists specializing in pediatrics are in private practice. Because they are self-employed, they must provide their own health insurance, life insurance, and retirement benefits.

Training and Other Qualifications for Dentists

All dentists must be licensed to practice in the United States. To qualify for a license in most states, candidates must graduate from a dental school accredited by the Commission on Dental Accreditation and pass written and practical examinations. Candidates may fulfill the written part of the state licensing by passing the National Board Dental Examinations. Currently, about 15 states require pediatric dentists to obtain a specialty license before practicing as a specialist. Requirements include two to four years of graduate education and, in some cases, completion of a special state examination. Most state licenses permit dentists to engage in both general and pediatric practices.

For admission into most dental schools, a minimum of two years of college predental education (courses in both the sciences and humanities) is required. However, the majority of dental students have at least a bachelor's degree. All dental schools require applicants to take the Dental Admissions Test (DAT). When selecting students, the schools consider scores earned on the DAT, the applicant's overall grade point average, science course grades, and information gathered through recommendations and interviews.

Dental school generally lasts four academic years. Studies begin with classroom instruction and laboratory work in basic sciences. Beginning courses in clinical sciences, including laboratory technique courses, also are provided at this time. During the last two years, the student gains practical experience by treating patients, usually in dental clinics under the supervision of licensed dentists. Most dental schools award the degree of Doctor of Dental Surgery.

Dentists specializing in pediatric dentistry must, of course, like children. Dentistry also requires diagnostic ability, good visual memory, excellent judgment of space and shape, and a high degree of manual dexterity, as well as scientific ability. Dentists who are in private practice also need good business skills.

What Being a Pediatric Dental Hygienist Is Like

Pediatric dental hygienists provide preventive dental care and teach children how to practice good oral hygiene. They show children how to brush and floss their teeth. Depending on the legal restrictions in the state where they work, hygienists provide a wide range of services. They examine children's teeth and mouths, recording the presence of diseases or abnormalities. They remove calculus, stain, and plaque from above and below the gumline; apply cavity-preventive agents such as fluorides and pit and fissure sealants; expose and develop dental x-rays; place temporary fillings and periodontal dressings; remove sutures; and polish and recontour amalgam restorations. Dental hygienists use a variety of instruments in the course of their work. They use hand and rotary instruments to clean teeth, x-ray machines to take dental pictures, syringes with needles to administer local anesthetics, and models of teeth to explain oral hygiene.

Pediatric dental hygienists work in offices and clinics. On the job they wear safety glasses, surgical masks, and gloves to protect themselves from infectious diseases. They must follow all health safeguards, which include strict adherence to proper radiological procedures, compliance with recommended aseptic technique, and utilization of appropriate protective devices when administering anesthetic gas.

Flexible scheduling is a distinctive part of being a dental hygienist. They may work full time or part time and in evenings or on weekends. Dentists frequently hire hygienists to work only two or three days a week.

The Personal Story of a Pediatric Dental Hygienist

Marcia Bozic is an active member of her husband's dental team as a registered dental hygienist. Every two years, she must take 12 hours of classes to keep her license current. Marcia had one year of college before she applied for admission to a dental hygienist program. She then studied in a university dental hygiene program for three years and graduated with a bachelor's degree in public health dental hygiene.

Marcia sees young patients who are scheduled for 30- to 45-minute appointments for cleaning, x-rays, fluoride treatment, and dental education. She likes working with children because it is so much fun to talk with them. And when children walk out of the office, they are wearing rings and carrying stickers and new toothbrushes along with their dental report cards, which describe how well they are doing in brushing their teeth and indicate what treatment has been done and what needs to be done. The dental progress report card can be seen in Figure 8.1.

Salary and Fringe Benefits

Earnings of dental hygienists are affected by where they live, their employment setting, and their education and experience. Dental hygienists who work in private dental offices may be paid on an hourly, daily, salary, or commission basis.

According to the American Dental Association, the average weekly wage for dental hygienists working 32 hours a week or more in a private practice was about $759 in 1995. Fringe benefits vary substantially by practice setting and may not be available for part-time hygienists. Dental hygienists who work for school systems, public health agencies, the federal government, or state agencies usually have substantial benefits.

Training and Other Qualifications for a Dental Hygienist

Dental hygienists must be licensed by the state in which they practice. To qualify for a license, it is essential to graduate from an accredited dental hygiene school and pass both a written and a clinical examination. In 1991, 205 programs in dental hygiene were accredited by the Commission on Dental Accreditation. Although some programs lead to a bachelor's degree, most grant an associate's degree. Six universities offer master's degree programs in dental hygiene. Completion of an associate's degree program is sufficient for practice in a private dental office.

About half of the dental hygiene programs prefer applicants who have completed at least one year of college. Some of the bachelor's degree programs require applicants to have completed two years. Requirements will vary from school to school. These schools offer laboratory, clinical, and classroom instruction.

Figure 8.1   Dental Progress Report Card

DENTAL PROGRESS REPORT
Dentistry for Children

Tooth Brushing GRADE (Plaque Score)		
AREAS OF DECAY		
OCCLUSION-Normal		
MALOCCLUSION	a. Skeletal	
	b. Dental (Crowding)	
	c. Minor Orthodontic (Future)	
	d. Major Orthodontic (Future)	
SOFT TISSUE (Gums, Tongue, Lips, etc.)	a. Normal	
	b. Inflamed	

The following treatment was completed today:

1. Examination	
2. Prophylaxis (Cleaning)	
3. Fluoride Treatment (Topical)	
4. Fluoride Treatment (Gel)	
5. Radiographs (X-Rays)	
6. Plaque Removal Instructions	
7. Dental Flossing Instructions	
8. Plaque Disclosing	

Recommendations:

1. Improve (Tooth Brushing)	
2. Plastic Sealants	
3. Restorations (Fillings)	
4. Daily Use of Dental Floss	
5. Disclosing Solution	
6. Daily Use of Fluoride Mouthwash	

Your next checkup appointment should be in:

☐ _____ Months _____

Name _____

Figure 8.1   Dental Progress Report Card (continued)

Grading Scale

UPPER
TEETH

RIGHT ☐   FRONT ☐   LEFT ☐

LOWER
TEETH

RIGHT ☐   FRONT ☐   LEFT ☐

The areas marked in Red are those areas of plaque missed when brushing. Your grade depends on the amount of plaque on your teeth.

No Plaque......................................=3 Points

$^1/_3$ Plaque ....=2 Points

$^2/_3$ Plaque ....=1 Point

All Covered ....=0 Point

Your Grade

A ....15–18 Very Good

B ....12–14 Good

C ....8–11 Average—try harder

D ....4–7 Almost failing

F...............0–3 Failing

THE AREAS MARKED IN RED INDICATE TEETH TO BE FILLED.

PRIMARY TEETH

NO DECAY ☐   UPPER

R I G H T

L E F T

LOWER

PERMANENT TEETH

NO DECAY ☐   UPPER

R I G H T

L E F T

LOWER

REMEMBER—A Bright Healthy Smile Depends on YOU!

Certain personal qualifications are essential for this profession. Dental hygienists need to work well with others, particularly children, who may be very apprehensive about dentistry. Personal neatness, cleanliness, and good health are additional important qualities hygienists need. Because they use dental instruments with little room for error within children's mouths, they must also have good manual dexterity.

PEDIATRIC PROFESSIONALS WHO COUNSEL CHILDREN

Some children are so unhappy and distressed that their friends, parents, and teachers are unable to help them resolve their problems. These children may need special help from a psychiatrist, psychologist, or counselor in order to get their lives back on track and face the future confidently. These professionals are highly trained individuals with years of postgraduate education. Many specialize in the treatment of children and devote most if not all of their practice to children.

Child Psychiatrists

Child psychiatrists deal primarily with children who may need more than advice and a chance to talk things over. Psychologists and counselors cannot prescribe drugs in the treatment of serious problems or disorders; only psychiatrists can. A common example of psychiatric medication is a drug given to treat attention deficit disorder (ADD). Child psychiatrists also use drugs in the treatment of schizophrenia, Tourette's syndrome, depression, sleeping difficulties, and bed-wetting problems.

Child psychiatrists are medical doctors who have taken three or more years of training in psychiatry after graduating from medical school. Psychiatrists generally work in private practice, clinics, or hospitals. Child psychiatry is a very small specialty field.

Child Psychologists

Child psychologists provide mental health services to children in schools, private settings, clinics, and hospitals. They help mentally and emotionally disturbed children adjust to life. They also assist children in dealing with stressful situations such as parental divorce, arrival of a sibling, and death of a family member or friend. Child psychologists counsel children, give diagnostic tests, provide individual, family, and group psychotherapy, and implement behavior modification programs. They may collaborate with doctors and other specialists in developing plans for treatment. More than one-third of all child psychologists work primarily in elementary and secondary schools. Many child psychologists work evenings and weekends to accommodate the schedules of school children and their parents.

Child psychologists in clinical settings or private practice usually have doctoral degrees, which require from three to five years of graduate work. A master's degree is required for school psychologists who concentrate on testing and counseling children. Competition for admission to both master's and doctoral programs is keen; some universities require an undergraduate degree in psychology for admission. Psychologists who offer any type of patient care must meet licensing or certification requirements of the state in which they are practicing.

Even more so than in other child care occupations, child psychologists must be emotionally stable, mature, and able to deal with people. Sensitivity, compassion, and the ability to inspire children are particularly important for clinical work and counseling. Patience and perseverance are also needed, since the results of psychological treatment often are slow to appear.

Counselors

Like child psychiatrists and psychologists, counselors cannot do therapy with children unless they are licensed by the state in which they practice. Many hold a MFCC (Marriage, Family, and Child Counselor) or similar license that requires them to have a master's degree in counseling or related areas and 3,000 hours of internship experience, half of which must be earned after completion of a master's degree. The time required to complete a master's degree and go on to become a licensed counselor is typically five to six years.

Many counselors focus their practice on families and children. A children's counselor will help the children of divorcing parents work out their feelings through art, games, role playing, and talking. Or a counselor may help an aggressive boy who is hitting others learn to explore other options for reacting when he is angry at another child. Children's counselors also work with children who are depressed, who don't know how to make friends, who have low self-esteem, who have been sexually or physically abused, and who must learn how to cope with learning disabilities. They may also be called upon in child custody cases to make recommendations. Counselors of children have the goal of giving children the tools and skills to cope with their current problems, so that they have a better chance of becoming healthy adults.

The Personal Story of a Counselor

Bill Shryer's interest in counseling actually began when he was in high school and started working in the psychiatric unit of a hospital. Since then, every career move and every educational degree has helped him become an expert counselor. One of his first degrees, a bachelor's in social work, showed him how social workers deal with personal, family, and community problems. It was, however, his stint in the navy as a neuropsychiatric technician and later work as a psychiatric nurse that gave him a sound medical background. Bill is one counselor who truly understands the role of medication in helping disturbed children and is able to work knowledgeably with the psychiatrists who dispense medicines to many of his patients. While obtaining a master's degree in social work, Bill was fortunate to have as his mentor Judith Wallerstein, who became famous for her study of the effects of divorce on children. Participating in the gathering of data for this study gave him a solid understanding of children's reactions to divorce. To complete preparation for his career, Bill became a Licensed Clinical Social Worker (LCSW) and a Board Certified Diplomate in clinical social work (BCD).

Today, Bill manages three attention deficit disorder clinics and handles the more disruptive behaviors of childhood and adolescence. While part of his day is necessarily devoted to business activities, he typically spends six hours a day in counseling.

Bill's specialty is counseling children; however, he does frequently see children and their parents together. Most patients attend 45-minute sessions once a week for six months or less. Then the visits taper down to one or two a month until the problems have been resolved. Bill considers his counseling part of a package. He works closely with pediatricians, social workers, family doctors, psychiatrists, and school districts advocating for children's legal rights under PL94-142, the federal law that provides special education services for all handicapped students.

Like truly effective people in every career, Bill is constantly educating himself on new discoveries in his field so he can implement them in his work. He is particularly fascinated by neurobiology and recent evidence that really disruptive behaviors are brain driven, not will driven. His career has become even more satisfying as genetic research now shows that many problems that confront children are based on nature, not nurture.

SPEECH-LANGUAGE PATHOLOGISTS

Speech-language pathology is a career area that deals specifically with improving children's speech. Speech-language pathologists work with children who stutter, lisp, cannot pronounce sounds correctly, or have some other problem with their speech. They assess children's speech difficulties and develop and carry out treatment programs. They work in hospitals, clinics, schools, private practices, or group practices. They are most likely to be employed in a school setting. Within schools, speech-language pathologists may work with just one child or with a small group of children. They will go into classrooms occasionally to help teachers with activities that meet the special needs of children with speech disorders. No matter where they work, part of their job involves counseling parents and instructing them in ways they can help their children.

A master's degree is necessary to work as a speech-language pathologist. Not all states require licenses for practicing in this field; however, those that do have very demanding licensing requirements that may include a master's degree or equivalent, 275 to 300 hours of supervised clinical experience, a passing score on a national examination, and nine months of postgraduate professional experience. License renewal depends on fulfilling continuing education requirements.

The employment picture is excellent for speech-language pathologists who work in health care settings, as the health care industry is continually growing. Jobs within the school setting are growing only at an average rate. The average salary for speech-language pathologists with one to three years' experience is approximately $38,000 a year according to the American Speech-Language-Hearing Association.

THE CHILDREN'S HOSPITAL AS A WORKPLACE

One setting where many health care professionals work together to care for children is a children's hospital. These hospitals are equipped to address the entire spectrum of children's health care needs, from preventive care to intensive treatment of injury or illness. One of these hospitals is the Lucile Salter Packard Children's Hospital at Stanford. The mission of this hospital is to serve all the children of the community who need its special services regardless of their means. The hospital has 1,300 full-time staff positions, consisting of:

Nursing and patient care support personnel

Professional services (laboratory, pharmacy, radiology, etc.) personnel

Support services (housekeeping, engineering, dietary, etc.) personnel

Administrative and support staff personnel

Physicians

The hospital promotes family-centered care and encourages parents to stay with their children 24 hours a day. The staff provides support services for patients and parents, including:

Social services

Interpreters (more than 30 languages)

Recreation therapy

Family health library

Chaplain

Occupational therapy

Physical therapy

Respiratory care

Nutrition services

Nursing

Hospital school

These descriptions of staff and services at the Lucile Salter Packard Children's Hospital at Stanford clearly illustrate the range of jobs within the health care profession that deal with children in a hospital setting.

HEALTH CARE PROFESSIONALS ARE HELD IN HIGH ESTEEM

All health care professionals are held in high esteem for the valued services they provide. And those who care for children are especially appreciated for wielding their skills in helping children recover from illnesses, injuries, and accidents, as well as in helping them stay healthy. Careers in this area are infinitely satisfying.

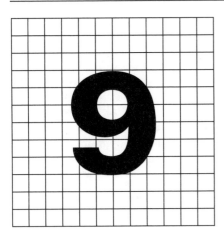

CAREERS ENSURING THE WELFARE OF CHILDREN

The welfare of the 70 million children in the United States has been steadily improving due to the efforts of people working in the areas of child welfare and juvenile justice. Unfortunately, there are still children living in homes where they are abused or neglected by their parents. There are also children whose anti-social behavior has brought them in conflict with their families, friends, society, and the law. They are gang members, runaways, truants, and children who commit crimes ranging from misdemeanors to major felonies. People who want to secure better lives for these children can find jobs as social workers, police officers, foster parents, juvenile-court judges, probation officers, juvenile-court referees, and child advocates.

SOCIAL WORKERS

Social workers help children and their families cope with problems. They provide direct counseling, give concrete information when it is needed, coordinate the services children require, remove children from dangerous situations, and make decisions about the placement of children in foster homes, group homes, and special-care facilities. They also facilitate adoptions.

Most social workers who want to work with children specialize in a single field such as child welfare and family services, children's protective services, or school services. The duties they perform may overlap between fields, and agencies will assign duties differently depending on staff size. The following paragraphs provide brief descriptions of social workers' responsibilities in each field.

Child welfare and family services. Social workers in this field counsel children who have difficulty adjusting socially. For example, if children are having serious problems in school, social workers consult with parents, teachers, and counselors to identify the underlying causes. Some social workers in this field arrange adoptions and help find foster homes for neglected or abandoned children. Also, social workers may work in residential institutions for children.

Children's protective services. These social workers investigate reports of child abuse and neglect and intervene when necessary. They may institute legal action to remove victims from homes and place them temporarily in an emergency shelter or with a foster family. Social workers may also be involved in reuniting children with their parents, overseeing the care of children in foster homes, and permanently placing children who have been removed from their parents' care.

School services. Social workers in this division diagnose students' problems and arrange needed services, counsel children in trouble, and integrate handicapped students into the general school population. They commonly deal with problems concerning misbehavior in class and excessive absences. School-services social workers also advise teachers on how to handle problem students.

Working Conditions and Employment

Social workers are employed in both the private and public sectors. In the private sector, jobs in social work that involve children can be found in social service agencies, community and religious organizations, adoption and foster care agencies, and hospitals. The vast majority of social workers in the United States, however, are employed by government agencies. In general, social workers in these agencies have jobs at the county level and in cities or suburbs.

The standard workweek for a social worker is 40 hours. These hours, however, can easily extend to evenings and weekends in order to deal with crisis situations and to meet with children and their parents. Furthermore, because of chronic budgetary constraints, many agencies are now understaffed, and social workers frequently find themselves handling huge caseloads.

Being a social worker who deals with children can be a pressure-packed job. There just may not be enough time to handle cases involving children's futures as in depth as the social worker desires. The work can also be emotionally draining, as social workers try to find the best solutions for children with very serious, even life-threatening problems. At the same time, the work is always satisfying because social workers do improve the lives of many troubled children.

Job Opportunities and Salaries

The employment of social workers is expected to increase faster than the average for all occupations through 2006. The need for social workers who are concerned with families in crisis is expected to grow. The employment of school-services social workers will expand in the years ahead in response to the adjustment problems of immigrants, children from single-parent families, and others in difficult situations. In addition, continued emphasis on integrating handicapped children into the general school population will probably lead to even more jobs for school-services social workers.

Future social workers need to realize that competition for jobs in cities is much stronger than in rural areas, which often find it difficult to attract and retain qualified staff.

Social work does not pay well, considering the level of education needed to enter the field. Social workers, who must hold at least a bachelor's degree, do not make as much money as teachers, who are required to reach similar education levels and who work significantly fewer hours. In 1997, social workers with bachelor's degrees had median earnings of $25,000, while those with master's degrees earned about $35,000.

Qualifications

The minimum requirement for almost every position as a social worker is a bachelor's degree, and the preferred degree is one in social work. A bachelor's degree in social work (B.S.W.) prepares graduates for direct service positions such as caseworker or group worker. Candidates for B.S.W. take courses in social work practice, social welfare policies, human behavior and the social environment, and social research methods. In addition, accredited B.S.W. programs require at least 400 hours of supervised field experience.

In some areas, especially in small communities, it may be possible to secure a job as a social worker with a degree in psychology, sociology, or a related field. However, educational requirements for entry-level positions are becoming more stringent. In many cities, only applicants with master's degrees in social work are being considered for openings.

To obtain supervisory positions in agencies with a large number of social workers, a master's degree in social work (M.S.W.) has almost become a prerequisite for career advancement. An M.S.W. prepares social workers to perform assessments, manage cases, and supervise other social workers. Master's programs usually take two years to complete and include 900 hours of supervised field instruction or internship. It is not essential to have a bachelor's degree in social work to be admitted to a master's program; however, undergraduate courses in psychology, biology, sociology, economics, political science, history, social anthropology, urban studies, and social work are recommended. Some schools offer an accelerated M.S.W. program to students who have a bachelor's degree in social work.

Every state has licensing, certification, or registration laws regarding the practice of social work and the use of professional titles. Standards for licensing vary by state. Voluntary certification is offered by the National Association of Social Workers (NASW), which grants the ACSW (Academy of Certified Social Worker) or ACBSW (Academy of Certified Baccalaureate Social Worker) and advanced credentials in clinical social work and school social work to those who qualify. Credentials are especially important for social workers in private practice, as some health insurance providers require social workers to have them to be reimbursed.

The Personal Story of a Social Worker in Children's Protective Services

Nick Costa has been a social worker for over 10 years. His bachelor's degree is in social work, and he is a NASW-certified social worker. Nick's career path clearly demonstrates the competition that exists for jobs in social work. In the metropolitan area where he lives, entry-level social workers at the department of social services must have a master's degree, preferably in social work, or five years of experience in order to work with children. Not having the qualifications for a job at the local department of social services, Nick found a job as a social worker at a private mental health agency that contracted with the county to provide services to the mentally ill. For two years, he worked with mentally ill adults in a program designed to mainstream clients out of mental hospitals and board-and-care facilities. Nick had learned about this job through his counselor at school, which demonstrates the importance of networking as a tool for finding jobs in social work.

Nick's next job was in a rural county close to where he lived. He found out about the opening for a social worker in the children's protective services (CPS) department by calling a job hot line. Because competition is intense, Nick prepared very carefully for the interview by talking to social workers in CPS, who described exactly what the job entailed. The preparation paid off, and he was hired to work in a small, overworked CPS department, even though he had no experience in this area. He began by reading case files and received on-the-job training from his supervisor and coworkers. He learned how to investigate reports of child abuse, monitor children's placements in foster homes, and write court reports.

After five years of employment as a social worker, Nick applied for a job in the county where he lived, as he now had the requisite experience to be hired. After several years of working in children's protective services in this county, he wanted to advance to a position as a supervisor. As a master's degree was required for the position, Nick began investigating where he could obtain a supervisory position without a master's degree. He found a job through a newspaper advertisement and hopes to advance to a supervisory position in the near future.

Nick's career path as a social worker shows the need to have a master's degree in order to advance to supervisory positions at many social service agencies. Because social workers have such heavy caseloads, it is difficult to combine work and getting a master's degree. The larger an agency is, the greater the opportunity for advancement. The following career ladder shows the progression of positions for social workers in large county agencies:

> director of welfare
> deputy director of welfare
> division manager
> supervisor
> social worker

Supervisors typically oversee the work of six to eight social workers in a particular program, while division managers guide the work of several supervisors. The higher social workers climb on the career ladder, the further they get from working directly with children.

Aptitudes

Social workers who deal with children make decisions that directly affect the quality of life many of their young charges will experience in the future. In order to make these extremely important decisions, social workers should be emotionally mature, objective, and sensitive to children and their problems. They must be able to handle responsibility, work independently, and maintain good working relationships with children and their caregivers and with fellow social workers. In addition, social workers need to have the following job-related skills and capacities:

- They must be familiar with the resources available in their community to help children.

- They must be reliable, so the children know that they will visit when they say they will.

- They must model correct behaviors for children.

- They must understand and be able to explain the juvenile court system.

- They must have an excellent memory for names, as they will deal with large numbers of children as well as other professionals who are working with the children.

- They must persuade the children, parents, foster parents, and counselors to act like a team.

- They must promptly return calls.

- They must be able to write clearly so that others can understand what they mean to say.

Specific Social Work Jobs Involving Children

Social-welfare agencies at the county level organize their programs dealing with children in different ways. Social workers may work in just one program, in two programs, or in one large umbrella program. The names of the programs and the exact nature of each will vary throughout the country. Examples of individual programs include the following:

Emergency response. Social workers respond to emergency calls that a child is being abused or neglected. The social workers must decide whether the child needs to be removed from his or her home. Interviews with the child, professionals who know the child (teachers, counselors, doctors), neighbors, and the child's parents are frequently used in the decision-making process. Reports are filed on the disposition of each case.

Reunification. Social workers manage the reunification of children with their families after they have been removed from their parents' care. The children are visited by the social worker in foster homes or in homes of relatives. The children's temporary caregivers are counseled on the care of the children. Meanwhile, social workers also monitor the parents' progress in counseling and parenting classes. Progress reports are written to the courts detailing the reunification status of each family.

Family maintenance. Children who have been made wards of the court are permitted to remain with their families in family maintenance programs. Social workers visit the homes and check with counselors on the progress that is being made to improve the home situation.

Permanency planning. When family reunification programs fail, social workers must develop a case plan and make recommendations to the court for the permanent placement of the child. Some children will be adopted. Others will live with relatives, guardians, or foster parents.

Adoption programs. Social workers investigate the background of the prospective parents and the child to be adopted. Based on their investigations, they make recommendations to the court.

What Being a Social Worker in Children's Protective Services Is Like

Social workers who work in child protection are sometimes the highest-paid because the job is so stressful. These professionals have to determine whether an abused child should remain in the home or be removed. This is not an easy decision to make, even after very careful assessment of a situation, because there are so many unknown factors involved. In addition, the decisions social workers make may be monitored by the press.

Mary Doyle is a county social worker in children's protective services in a large metropolitan area. Her usual caseload is from 12 to 20 families; she considers 15 ideal.

Unfortunately, children's protective services social workers usually do not begin to work with a family until after the abuse or neglect has taken place and has been reported. Mary attempts to protect children from physical and sexual abuse and neglect. Families are required by law to work with social workers when reports of child abuse have been filed by nurses, doctors, teachers, relatives, neighbors, or others.

Mary does very little counseling. She meets with a family, carefully assesses the situation, and develops a case plan. She tries to get the family to agree on objectives and refers them to whatever services they need, which often include counseling. Then she monitors the situation in order to assess how the family is doing. While the aim is to keep families together, at times Mary must have children removed from their homes to ensure their safety. When this happens, Mary must testify in court.

Reflecting on her career with children's protective services, Mary says, "This is a necessary job; someone must do it. You can't say that about all jobs." As a social worker, she sees people who have been victimized by the system. "It is hard to be a stellar parent when you are impoverished," she says. Mary believes that social workers have a mandate not just to help individuals but also to change society and institutions that may be oppressive.

What Being a Social Worker in Adoption Services Is Like

Some children become dependents of the state because parental rights to the children have been terminated by the courts. These high-risk children—abused, abandoned, neglected, or handicapped—are the ones for whom Ed Holt tries to find families. His entire department celebrated when a worker in Ed's unit found a skilled family for an infant who was severely disabled and retarded because of a rare medical condition that required ongoing medical help.

Ed is unit supervisor of adoption services for a county and holds a master's degree in social work. Social workers in his unit have three specific duties. First, they become the child's guardian and make an assessment of the child's adoption needs. After the child is adopted, they make sure things are going well until the adoption is finalized. Second, these social workers study the home to determine what it is like, and they try to match parents and child. Third, they make a genetic search to determine a child's background so that the child and both parents can locate each other, if they wish, after the child is 19 years old.

Previously, Ed worked in children's protective services for 12 years, and positive feedback came from his coworkers rather than the families with whom he worked. Now he is involved in major life events for children and their families. When all the pieces come together and the children and families find permanence that they might not have achieved without his help, Ed's career satisfaction is immense.

POLICE OFFICERS IN YOUTH SERVICES

The primary work of police officers is the safety of the country's cities, towns, and highways. Police officers, however, are also involved in working with young people in trouble—runaways, gang members, abused children, and children suspected of committing crimes. They also work as liaison officers with schools, teaching children about personal and traffic safety and substance abuse. In small communities and rural areas, youth work is often just part of the wide range of a police officer's duties. By contrast, large police departments usually assign officers to youth services departments where they may work in just one area—for example, as a school liaison or in a gang outreach program. Most officers find considerable satisfaction in working with youths. For example, a school liaison officer may see a big downturn in drug activity after presenting a comprehensive drug program at a middle school. Or fights between gangs may diminish because of a youth services officer's efforts to involve gang members in athletic programs.

Job Outlook and Earnings

The escalation of juvenile crime and the higher incidence of child abuse have led to a greater need for police officers in youth services departments. This demand is increased even more by the current emphasis on school liaison work by police officers. Nevertheless, employment growth in youth services (as well as in other police departments) is tempered by budgetary constraints. The number of job opportunities will vary from year to year and from place to place. Overall, the employment of police officers is expected to increase about as fast as the average for all occupations through 2006.

The median salary of nonsupervisory police officers is about $35,000, while supervisory officers earn more than $41,000. Total earnings can be much higher due to payments for overtime. Earnings vary by region and the size of the police department. Larger police departments usually pay higher salaries. Furthermore, police officers who work in the West earn somewhat higher salaries, while those employed in the South earn somewhat less.

Police officers receive common fringe benefits such as paid vacation, sick leave, and medical and life insurance. In addition, most police departments provide officers with special allowances for uniforms. Because police officers are generally covered by liberal pension plans, many are able to retire after 20 or 25 years of work experience at half pay.

Qualifications

Individuals do not apply to become officers in specific police departments, but rather to become police officers. After becoming a police officer, they may then be assigned to youth services or may apply to the department when openings occur.

Candidates for police positions must usually be U.S. citizens and at least 20 years of age. Eligibility for appointment as a police officer typically depends on performance in the following areas:

- Competitive written examinations

- Physical examinations, often including tests of vision, strength, and agility

- Oral interviews

- A polygraph test

- Drug testing

- A background check

In some departments, prospective police officers are also given personality tests and may be interviewed by a psychiatrist or a psychologist. Candidates who successfully pass the required tests are then placed on an eligibility list.

Applicants must usually have a high school education. A few police departments accept applicants as recruits who have less than a high school education, particularly if they have worked in a field related to law enforcement. Many departments, however, are now requiring some college training, especially in law enforcement.

The Personal Story of a Youth Services Police Officer

Detective Robin Heinemann is a detective in the juvenile bureau of a large suburban police department. Her childhood dream was to be involved in law enforcement in some way—a dream she began to work on early in her life. By the time she was in eighth grade, she had joined a Law Explorers group, similar to a scout troop. And after high school, she joined a small police department and worked as a reserve officer while she attended college. When Robin was 23, she passed the requisite tests and became an officer in the police department where she currently works. She worked on patrol for four years before applying for and getting her present position in the juvenile bureau, where she works from 8:00 A.M. to 5:00 P.M. Monday through Friday.

In her work at the juvenile bureau, Robin handles a load of 50 to 60 cases at a time. Her cases are generated by a patrol officer at the scene or a citizen making a report to the front desk. She handles cases on a priority basis. Many of the cases involve children who are in middle school. Each case has to be carefully investigated. She often talks to the children involved while they are at school rather than at home. Many of the cases that she handles deal with child abuse. Robin has to establish the facts, corroborate all statements, and put all the facts together to substantiate the allegation. If there is a crime, she writes up a report that goes to the district attorney, who decides on future action based on the evidence Robin presented. In the case of in-home molestation, Robin works with a social worker to take a child from his or her home. Social workers have the authority to place children in protective custody if a police officer signs the appropriate document. Robin follows every case that she handles through to the end. Some cases may only involve a little paperwork, while others may involve extensive investigative interviews. Some will end in the conviction of an adult. Besides handling her caseload, Robin also works as a school liaison officer. In this assignment, she presents programs on safety and substance abuse to school children.

Robin is well trained for her work through special seminars and in-service training in such subjects as interviews and interrogations and sexual assault and child abuse. In addition, during the course of her police career she has obtained an associate's degree in justice administration, a bachelor's degree in criminal justice administration, and a master's degree in public administration. Other police officers in the youth bureau have similar educational backgrounds.

Because of her interest in children, Robin wants to get more education in child psychology. Her ultimate goal is to obtain a doctorate and become an administrator in the police department.

CAREERS WITHIN THE JUVENILE JUSTICE SYSTEM

The major careers in this area are as juvenile-court judges, juvenile-court referees, caseworkers, and lawyers. Volunteers may serve as court-appointed special advocates for children. Each state sets up its own juvenile justice system according to the laws of the state; therefore, job titles as well as responsibilities will vary from state to state. Because juvenile justice is only a small part of the entire judicial system, having a full-time career in this area is usually only possible in cities and large metropolitan areas. Unfortunately, the increase in crimes against juveniles and serious crimes committed by juveniles have led to an increased need for career professionals in juvenile justice.

What Being a Juvenile-Court Judge Is Like

Experience in the practice of law is required, or at least strongly preferred, for most judgeships. The first step, becoming a lawyer, is a difficult and time-consuming undertaking. In nearly every state, prospective lawyers have to pass a bar examination and a separate written ethics examination. And to qualify for the bar examination, it is necessary to have completed at least three years of college and graduated from a law school approved by the American Bar Association or the proper state authorities. The difficulty of becoming a lawyer is heightened because the competition for admission to law school is intense. Furthermore, after individuals have become experienced lawyers, they face stiff competition to become a judge, as so much prestige is associated with the position. Increasing concern about crime and juveniles should spur the demand for judges; on the other hand, tight public funding may slow job growth.

The process of becoming a juvenile-court judge is different in every state. Judges are typically elected or appointed to this position. In large cities and metropolitan areas, many judges concentrate solely on juvenile justice; in rural areas, judges may deal with juvenile cases only one day a month.

Juvenile-court judges have jurisdiction in three areas:

1. *Delinquency cases* involve juveniles who have committed crimes from shoplifting to major felonies. Certain felonies, such as armed robbery and murder, are often transferred to the adult court system.

2. *Dependency cases* involve juveniles who have had crimes committed against them, such as abuse or neglect.

3. *Status offenses* involve acts legally prohibited to juveniles that would not be a crime if committed by an adult. Included in these acts are being a runaway, incorrigible behavior, smoking, drinking, and truancy.

The goal of juvenile justice is rehabilitation. Judges weigh public safety and individual rights in making their decisions regarding the disposition of cases.

Responsibilities of Juvenile-Court Judges

In juvenile court, judges have overwhelming responsibilities in making decisions that directly affect the lives of children. On one side, they are handling abuse and neglect cases in which they decide whether children should be removed from or returned to their families, and what services should be offered to those families. On the other side, they are handling increasingly violent and drug-related crimes committed by children, trying to change delinquent children's lives while protecting the community.

The role of the juvenile-court judge also includes the following responsibilities:

- Making sure that all parties appearing before the court receive their legal and constitutional rights

- Ensuring that all the systems involved in bringing cases to court are working fairly and efficiently

- Making sure that there are an adequate number of lawyers, probation officers, police, and social workers to complete the work of the juvenile court

- Keeping abreast of the latest information on such subjects as child abuse, dysfunctional families, and substance abuse

- Exercising a leadership role in the community in determining the needs of at-risk families and providing for the development of services for these families

- Knowing how cases that do not reach the court are resolved

- Monitoring the progress of the child and families to see that the terms of court orders are being followed

- Managing the administration of the juvenile probation department and the juvenile court staff (in some cases)

What Being a Juvenile-Court Referee Is Like

The caseload many juvenile-court judges face is simply so large that assistance is required. Juvenile-court referees act as judges in resolving certain cases involving children. They hold preliminary hearings involving delinquent, abused, and neglected children and make recommending decisions. If the parties involved in the case do not agree with the referee's decision, they can appeal to a judge for review of the case. Qualifications for being a juvenile-court referee usually include holding a bachelor's degree in the social sciences and having related juvenile or casework experience.

What Being a Juvenile-Court Caseworker Is Like

Caseworkers in juvenile court supervise and counsel youths on probation. They also investigate the backgrounds of delinquent youths to help the judge or referee make the most appropriate disposition of a case. Both juvenile-court caseworkers and caseworker aides may supervise the licensing of foster homes and investigate adoptions. For both positions, related experience plus a bachelor's degree in the social sciences are desirable.

What Being a Children's Advocate Is Like

In describing the Court-Appointed Special Advocate program (CASA), Judge Salvatore T. Mulé, president of the National Council of Juvenile and Family Court Judges, said, "Abused and neglected children need someone to speak up for them. No one does this more effectively and with more dedication than the CASA volunteer. As a judge, I rely heavily on the CASA's insight and recommendation to the court. CASA does work."

Children can become lost in foster care for different reasons. CASA volunteers work to see that children do not fall through the cracks. They are trained volunteers who advise the court about the best interests of children. These volunteers work to ensure that a child's right to a safe, permanent home is acted on by the court in a sensitive and expedient manner. The volunteers conduct investigations and speak with many people—parents, teachers, doctors, neighbors, social workers, foster parents, and especially the child. They review all pertinent records and often become the most knowledgeable person about a child's situation. One of the reasons that the CASA volunteer is so effective is that social workers and attorneys work with many children, while the CASA volunteer is usually only involved with one child at a time. Almost 28,000 people are currently serving as CASA volunteers. Not only is being a volunteer an excellent opportunity to help children, it is also a solid way to gain experience in the juvenile justice system.

THE SATISFACTION OF SAFEGUARDING CHILDREN'S WELFARE

To work in child welfare or juvenile justice is to make a commitment to helping children who are abused, neglected, or caught in a life of antisocial behavior. They are not the "pretty" children seen on television sitcoms, but rather children who have seen the grim side of life. Working in child welfare or juvenile justice is a career in helping the most needy children. The larger dividend is the positive contribution that children whose lives have been turned around will be able to make to society in the future.

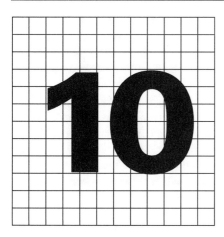

ARTS AND ENTERTAINMENT CAREERS WITH CHILDREN

A child's education is not complete unless it extends beyond the classroom into new arenas. While schools expose children to the arts, a true appreciation of art, music, dance, and theater is more likely to occur when children see performances or actively study one or more of the arts. Besides participating in and being entertained by different forms of the arts, children seek entertainment from television, books, and live performances of clowns and puppeteers. Many career options exist for those who wish to share their skills in the arts and entertainment with children.

CAREERS IN THE ARTS

Musicians can teach music to the neighborhood children as well as to prodigies at the Juilliard School. Artists can paint or sculpt images of children or teach children these skills. Actors can perform in children's theaters or introduce children to techniques of acting and performing on stage. Instructors are needed to teach dance to children wishing to learn ballet or ballroom dancing. All of these jobs involving children and the arts can be either full-time or part-time positions. While teachers of the arts can find employment at schools, there are also jobs at studios and in homes as teachers. Many individuals who teach children the arts are self-employed. Quite frequently, they will also work as musicians, artists, and performers. Their earnings depend on where they live, their experience, and their professional reputations.

What Being a Music Teacher Is Like

Teaching music is an excellent way to share a love of music with children—from fledgling musicians in preschool to skilled older children. Each age level offers different challenges and rewards. Prospective music teachers may wish to focus on a particular age group. The setting for teaching music to children can be elementary, junior high, middle, and high schools, studios, the children's homes, or the instructors' homes. Information about careers in teaching music can be obtained by contacting the Music Educators National Conference (MENC), 1806 Robert Fulton Drive, Reston, Virginia 20190. Additional information can be obtained through studying professional journals, including *The American Music Teacher, The American String Teacher, Music Educator's Journal,* and *The Choral Journal.*

Being a private music teacher is an excellent way for a musician to work closely with children. How many students a teacher will have depends on the demand for music instruction in the area as well as the individual's reputation as a skilled teacher. Since most students are in school during the day, a private teacher's workday does not normally begin until the end of the school day. Fees usually range from $15 to $50 per lesson, although some experts command fees as high as $150 per lesson.

Training. Many musicians who become teachers of young children began studying music at an early age themselves. Through their school years, they gained valuable experience playing in formal musical organizations and in small groups with their friends. Musicians need extensive and prolonged training to acquire the necessary skill, knowledge, and ability to interpret and teach music. This training may be obtained through private study with an accomplished musician, in a college or university music program, in a music conservatory, or through practice with a group. For study in an institution, an audition is frequently necessary. Formal courses include music theory, music interpretation, composition, conducting, and instrumental instruction. Many colleges, universities, and music conservatories grant bachelor's or higher degrees in music. Many also grant degrees in music education to qualify graduates for a state certificate to teach music in an elementary or secondary school.

The Personal Story of a Private Music Teacher

Melissa Williams has taught music in elementary school and has worked at a residential treatment center for emotionally disturbed children. Today, she teaches tuba, euphonium, and trombone to about 40 students, plays in symphony orchestras in two cities, and does some freelancing at recording studios making music tapes. To get started as a private teacher in a new city, she joined a brass choir and played with a local symphony, where she met many school music teachers who recommended her to students in their classes. In her free time, Melissa practices the tuba, hoping to win an audition to be a regular in a major symphony orchestra. To hone her skills, this accomplished musician takes lessons from an expert player with the Chicago Symphony. Her solid educational background in music includes a bachelor's degree in music with a minor in music therapy and a master's degree in performance.

What Being a Dance Teacher Is Like

Children just naturally dance; they can hardly keep their bodies still. Furthermore, they enjoy perfecting their skills through dance classes. Millions of dollars are spent every year for dance lessons for preschoolers learning tap dance and ballet to junior high school students learning social dancing. Teachers are needed to train all these eager dancers in a variety of settings, such as day care centers, public schools, dance schools, conservatories, studios, and special education programs. Teachers of this art form have the opportunity to actually dance with children as they do their job.

Aptitudes. Dance teachers need to be expert dancers who have teaching skills. The following aptitudes are needed to be a successful dance teacher:

- An anatomical understanding of how the body works
- Ability to relate to children of different ages
- Enjoyment of music
- Ability to choreograph dances for children
- Patience to teach the same step over and over
- Organizational skills needed to break a dance down into parts and then reteach each part until the whole dance has been mastered
- Skills necessary to keep discipline in a class
- A sense of rhythm
- Ability to express ideas, moods, and emotions through dance movements
- Self-confidence
- Creativity
- Ability to work under pressure
- Ambition
- Talent
- Willingness to spend long hours in training and practice
- Good physical endurance
- Leadership ability
- Sincere interest in teaching dance to children and a love of dancing

Training. The training and educational background needed to teach dance depends on the type of dance an instructor wishes to teach and where he or she wants to teach. Many private dance teachers have trained since early childhood, and their own personal background is the foundation of their teaching. Most of these dancers will continue their own lessons and practice sessions even after they have started to teach dance. To teach dance in a public school, it is necessary to have the same degrees and credentials that other teachers have. According to the American Dance Guild, the average salary of a teacher in private practice ranges from $11,000 to $33,000 a year.

What Being a Dance/ Movement Therapist Is Like

This career fits within both the arts and medical fields. Dance/movement therapists use the art of dance to improve the physical and emotional health of children with whom they are working. The American Dance Therapy Association defines dance/movement therapy as the use of movement as a process that furthers the emotional and physical integration of the individual. To become a dance/movement therapist, it is essential to complete both an undergraduate program with emphasis in psychology and training in a variety of dance forms, followed by professional training at the graduate level and an internship. Dance/movement therapists also need to be able to perform, choreograph, and teach dance.

The moving body is the medium of the dance/movement therapist's work. The therapist focuses on the communicative, expressive, and adaptive aspects of nonverbal behavior, using these to help clients effect changes in thinking, feelings, physical functioning, and behavior. The method consists of structuring and guiding bodily experience toward an expression of wholeness and self-awareness.

Most dance/movement therapists who are involved with children work in psychiatric hospitals and community health centers. Jobs are also available in hospitals, special schools, rehabilitation centers, developmental centers, and correctional facilities. This field is still relatively new, and therapists do not need a state license to practice. The American Dance Therapy Association distinguishes between therapists who are prepared to work within a team or under supervision and those who can work independently. Therapists with the title Dance Therapist Registered (DTR) have a master's degree and are fully qualified to work in a professional treatment system. Therapists with the title Academy of Dance Therapists Registered (ADTR) have met additional requirements and are fully qualified to teach, supervise, and practice privately.

What Being a Children's Artist Is Like

One of the few careers in the arts in which an artist can make a small profit is painting or sculpting children. This is an extremely small career field. Nevertheless, a few artists become famous for their representations of children and are able to earn an impressive income from their work. Mary Cassatt was one of these artists. One of America's most famous women painters, she is known for her pictures of mothers and children. Only the most successful artists are able to support themselves solely through the sale of their works. Many also work in galleries or in some administrative capacity related to the arts or teach art to support themselves.

CAREERS IN ENTERTAINMENT

Children are an appreciative audience. They thoroughly enjoy being entertained, whether it is by a clown at a children's birthday party, a television program, or a stage show. Competition for employment as an entertainer is keen. Many entertainers who focus primarily on entertaining children also have other jobs. There are, however, entertainers like Mister Rogers who work full time within this profession.

The Personal Story of a Magician

Steve Hart shows children a book about fishing, and a fish squirts water on him. When he displays a book about banking, money pops out. The book on Aladdin breathes smoke. Steve is a magician who gives reading motivational programs in schools and markets trade and sales shows for adults. His "Magic of Reading" show for children combines entertainment with the theme of reading. It is a fast-paced, thought-provoking program that encourages children to read and emphasizes the importance of the alphabet, words, and reading. And, of course, it begins with the magical books that he takes from his reading treasure chest. With a little more magic carefully applied during his performance, all the books in the chest turn to gold and Steve has sparked the children's interest in reading.

Steve started training to be a magician in fifth grade by practicing with the magician's kit his parents had given him and reading library books on magic tricks. According to Steve, the only schooling that is really helpful in becoming a magician is teaching yourself. First, future magicians study; then they must practice, practice, and practice until they gain skill. Excellent eye-hand coordination is a prerequisite of this profession, and a background in theater can make performances more dramatic. Steve points out that magicians can never stand still; they must always be improving and looking for new and exciting ways to entertain. Steve has invented several tricks, including one in which he makes a two-liter bottle of pop disappear right before an audience.

Being a magician is a very small career field. There are only about 1,000 full-time magicians in the country. Most are amateurs. Starting as a young magician, it is possible to earn from $25 to $50 for a performance. Full-time magicians like Steve will earn from $20,000 to $100,000 a year. Superstar magicians will earn even more.

Steve strongly advises anyone interested in magic to become a member of the International Brotherhood of Magicians (IBM). Members, who can be as young as 12, receive a monthly magazine, *Linking Ring*, devoted to the history of magic and the techniques involved in performing tricks. There is even a special section for young magicians. Local chapters of IBM, called "rings," have monthly meetings. There are also international conventions. Steve believes that it is very important for magicians to belong to a fellowship organization where it is possible to mix with other magicians.

Magicians are self-employed and must generate their own business or use an agent. Steve has an office in his home. He sends out many mailings and even publishes his own newsletter to find clients for his magic show.

The Personal Story of a Clown

Randy Blades is Krackles T. Clown. The *T* stands for *the*. After having his face painted as a clown at a magic convention, he looked in the mirror and decided to become a clown. As Krackles, Randy started making balloon animals for children and then worked a series of shows. Although there are clown schools and even a clown college, Randy is self-taught. In his first year as a clown he made only $10,000. He persevered, however, and today he is scarcely able to keep up with all the programs he is requested to give at child care centers, birthday parties, conventions, and television shows. Plus, he works at several restaurants each week on their family nights. For several years, he and Steve Hart, the magician mentioned earlier, had their own television show, *Wacky Morning Cartoon Club*.

Randy is usually in clown makeup four times a week. When he first started making up his face, he needed over an hour to complete the job. Now it only takes him 15 minutes. On a typical workday, Randy may perform at 9:00 A.M. and again at 10:15 A.M. at child care centers. Then he may be off to a birthday party at 1:00 P.M. followed by two more child care centers in the afternoon. In the evening, he may perform for adults at a corporate event.

What Being a Puppeteer Is Like

Everyone is familiar with the Muppets; however, puppeteers perform throughout the country in theaters and schools, on local television shows, at malls, and at children's parties. Some colleges actually have courses in the basics of puppeteering. Students can learn how to construct puppets and sets, make costumes, and handle the business side of this career. Working as an assistant to an established puppeteer is the best preparation for a career in puppetry. Special skills required in this profession include creativity, manual dexterity, knowledge of what will appeal to a particular audience, and a desire to entertain. Like clowns and magicians, puppeteers must spend considerable time soliciting business. The range of annual income for most puppeteers is between $8,000 to $50,000.

Careers in Television

Who can forget watching Captain Kangaroo talk to Mr. Greenjeans or Mister Rogers visit with Lady Elaine? Besides the many public and network television shows for children, many local stations also broadcast shows featuring homegrown television stars interacting on camera with children. This career field is very small and the competition for jobs is intense. Formal training in communications from a college or technical school can he helpful in getting a first job in this field, as can an internship at a local television station.

Careers in Publishing Children's Books

The books that children enjoy reading or having read to them are produced by authors, editors, and illustrators. While these professionals do not work directly with children, they do have the opportunity to create books that entertain and educate children. The book publishing industry is centered in New York and Chicago. Although authors and illustrators are typically self-employed and not required to live and work in these two cities, editors are usually employed by the book publishing companies located in these areas.

Author. Authors of children's books are creative and imaginative people who are familiar with what appeals to children. Unfortunately, few books are such bestsellers that they produce enough income for the author to live on, and very few authors are able to devote their careers solely to writing children's books. Besides writing the text, some authors also produce the illustrations for their books. Unless authors have contracts to produce books for a publishing house, they must contact, or have their agents contact, a number of publishers and attempt to sell each book they write. This task is much easier after authors have had one or more books published. Once their reputations have been established, writers find it easier to get publishers interested in looking at their latest books or ideas for books. No specific training is required to become an author. Most authors will learn their trade by continually writing.

Illustrator. Most illustrations for children's books are produced by freelance illustrators, although some illustrators work on the staff of book publishing firms. Illustrations play an important role in children's books and must tie in closely to the text. Illustrators must determine the point of view of the author and graphically present it to young readers. Furthermore, illustrators need to have thoroughly developed their technical skills, which they usually have done through training in college, university, and art-school classes. Although illustrators can succeed without formal training, most have bachelor's degrees. Today, there is considerable competition for illustrating jobs from other illustrators as well as desktop publishers and photographers who wish to illustrate books.

Freelance illustrators begin their careers by developing a portfolio of their work to show to editors. Until they develop a set of clients who regularly contract for their work, they may earn very little. Successful illustrators of children's books can earn high incomes and pick and choose the type of work they do.

Editor. The task of a children's book editor is to plan the contents of the books and to supervise their preparation. The editor decides what will appeal to young readers, finds authors to create these materials, and oversees production of the books. Editors hire writers and other employees, plan budgets, and negotiate contracts with freelance authors. They are often helped by assistants who check manuscripts for readability and style and review copy for errors in grammar, punctuation, and spelling.

Most editors have college degrees. They also need to be creative and have the ability to express ideas clearly and logically. The path to becoming an editor usually begins with the position of assistant editor, copyeditor, or production assistant. Because so many people want to be editors, competition is keen for entry-level positions in this field. Serving as an intern in a publishing house or finding a part-time job in publishing is a good stepping stone to a full-time job.

ARTS AND ENTERTAINMENT CAREERS ARE REWARDING

Arts and entertainment careers associated with children are immensely gratifying. They allow individuals to pursue the interests they truly enjoy and share these interests with children. Although this is not a large career area, it is an extremely satisfying one for creative individuals who wish to introduce children to the richness the arts and entertainment can bring to their lives.

MORE CAREERS WORKING WITH CHILDREN

The population of children in this country is at an all-time high. Furthermore, new products and companies devoted primarily to children are rapidly being created because of technological innovations. As a result of these changes, there are more careers than ever before in which people can work with or on the behalf of children. Some of these careers are very familiar, such as child care worker or teacher. Careers in health care, child welfare, and juvenile justice are also explored in this book, as are jobs designed to entertain children or teach them sports and recreational skills. There are also a number of less familiar and new careers in which people can spend their days in close contact with children. Some careers, like those of research scientist and educational-toy maker, can significantly impact the lives of children even though they involve little actual contact with children. This chapter describes more careers associated with children.

WHAT BEING A CHILDREN'S LIBRARIAN IS LIKE

Children's librarians work in large public libraries and school libraries/media centers. They work closely with children or perform tasks that promote children's interest in library materials and reading.

In large public libraries, a separate room is typically devoted to books, periodicals, and media for children. In this room, children's librarians help children find specific materials and make suggestions about books they might like to read. The librarians are also involved in programs with children of different age groups. The library's children's program may have storytelling times for young children, book clubs for older children, and special summer programs for school-age children. The librarians also devote time to creating and maintaining book lists on different topics for the children. A master's degree in library science (M.L.S.) with emphasis on children's services is necessary for almost every position as a children's librarian in public libraries. Some master's programs take one year to complete, while others take two years.

School librarians not only help children find the information they need and books they wish to read, they also play an important role in showing children how to use the library. Besides working in the library, they frequently visit classrooms to discuss books, research techniques, and library usage. In addition, school librarians help teachers develop their own book lists and acquire materials for classroom instruction. Most states require school librarians to be certified as teachers and to have taken courses in library science. To get a job in some schools, it is necessary to have a master's degree in library science or in education with a specialty in library school media or educational media.

Salaries of librarians vary according to their qualifications and the location of the library. Salaries of children's librarians average more than $35,000 in public libraries. In school libraries, librarians earn salaries similar to those of teachers. The demand for children's librarians is expected to grow more slowly than other occupations through 2006. Budgetary constraints in cities and schools are slowing the growth of employment opportunities for these librarians.

WHAT BEING A CHILDREN'S PHOTOGRAPHER IS LIKE

Many photographers specialize in an area involving children, such as children's portraits or school photographs. They may work for a commercial studio or be self-employed. They can be found working in studios, in booths at shopping malls, in children's homes or schools, or at any place that children gather for activities. Skilled photographers capture the essence of the children they are photographing. To do this, they must not only be skilled in the technical aspects of photography but must also have learned how to handle children ranging in age from infant to preteen. Good eyesight, artistic ability, creativity, and manual dexterity are also required.

There is no one best way to become an excellent photographer of children. Individuals considering a career in this field should subscribe to photography magazines and newsletters. Joining camera clubs or working in camera stores can be helpful. Learning on the job is often an effective approach for children's photographers. Attending a college, community college, vocational-technical institute, or a private trade and technical school that offers courses in photography is also useful in becoming a skilled photographer. Basic courses in photography will cover equipment, processes, and techniques. A bachelor's degree, however, will also give fledgling photographers of children a chance to take business courses in case they desire to be self-employed.

Only average growth is expected in the employment of portrait photographers. Salaried photographers average a salary of more than $30,000. Some self-employed photographers earn as much as $75,000; however, others earn less than $15,000.

WHAT BEING AN EMPLOYEE IN A CHILDREN'S MUSEUM IS LIKE

Many people regard museums as old and dusty places where they can view art, historical, or scientific objects. However, anyone who has ever visited a children's museum knows that they are lively, colorful places with many interactive displays. Children can be seen scampering through caves, riding turn-of-the-century carousels, and watching trains whiz around on a complicated maze of tracks. Unfortunately, children's museums are only found in major metropolitan areas.

Within a children's museum, as within all museums, there are jobs for archivists, curators, administrators, and their assistants. Each individual performs the same tasks that he or she would perform in most other museums, except that the collections in these museums are of items that interest children. The curators might plan and prepare exhibits of Barbie dolls, live turtles, or the inner workings of the heart. There might be interactive displays in which children can take their blood pressure or investigate how pulleys work. Curators oversee all the collections in the museum as well as acquire new items through purchases, gifts, field exploration, and intermuseum loans. The job of archivists in children's museums is to describe and organize the museum's collections so that individual items can be easily located.

To secure a job as a curator or an archivist, it is just about essential to have a graduate degree, and even then competition is keen as there are so few positions available in these areas. Many individuals have to work as interns, assistants, and even volunteers to get sufficient experience to obtain a job in a museum. Curators will often advance through several positions to become museum directors.

WHAT BEING A YOUTH MINISTER IS LIKE

People who choose careers as youth ministers are seeking to make a difference in children's lives. They also have deep personal faith. Their job consists of planning youth retreats, organizing and managing social functions for young members of their religious groups, and doing some counseling. Their work hours are rarely standard; they regularly work with young people after school, in the evenings, and on weekends.

Most youth ministers find jobs with large congregations. There are no specific requirements for this position; however, most youth ministers have bachelor's degrees in such areas as social work, education, and counseling. They should also have coursework in theology, psychology, and counseling. In some congregations, youth ministers will be priests, rabbis, or ordained ministers. The demand for youth ministers is high in areas that have large populations of young people.

WHAT BEING A SALESPERSON IN A CHILDREN'S RETAIL STORE IS LIKE

Each day millions of dollars are spent by children and their parents on products specifically designed for children. Salespeople who sell children's clothing, toys, sports equipment, books, videos, and learning materials have an opportunity to deal directly with children on many of their sales. They have to stay knowledgeable about the current fads and fancies of young people, which can change overnight. Salespeople also need to know how to communicate effectively with their young customers.

Those who wish to concentrate on selling products to children can find jobs in small specialty stores as well as specific departments in large stores. There is always a demand for salespeople because the turnover rate in these positions is high. There are no formal educational requirements to enter this field. Many people start working in sales as a first job before they even graduate from high school. Employers do want salespeople who enjoy working with children and have the patience and understanding to deal with them effectively. Tired children can be difficult customers.

For many salespeople, the starting salary is minimum wage. Salespeople can work for hourly wages, on commission, or for a combination of hourly wages and commissions. They will not usually receive benefits unless they work full time at large stores. Effective salespeople can become department managers and buyers.

WHAT BEING A CREATOR OF CHILDREN'S PRODUCTS IS LIKE

While individuals who create products for children generally do not work closely with children, they are still pursuing a career that directly benefits children. Children need clothing to wear and toys to play with. Designers of children's clothing will typically work for manufacturers or design lines of clothing for chain stores. Children's toys are constantly being updated, and new toys are created each year. Every one of these toys has been created by a toy designer. Some toy designers own their own companies while others work for major manufacturers of children's toys. Both the creators of children's clothing and toys need to understand the psychology of children—how children think and what they want. No formal education is required for these jobs. However, creativity and ingenuity are prerequisites to successful careers in both areas.

WHAT WORKING WITH CHILDREN AND COMPUTERS IS LIKE

With millions of children using computers and the Internet for both recreation and education, brand-new career opportunities are opening up for computer buffs. They can work directly with children, instructing them in the many ways there are to use the computer. Or they may work on-line answering children's questions about homework and other topics. However, the greatest demand in this area is for individuals who can develop computer programs and websites for children. With the Internet expanding so rapidly, they will find jobs at companies that did not exist just a few years or even months ago or perhaps start their own companies. These jobs require both a knowledge of children and computer expertise. Currently, there is also a need for computer buffs who can create filters to block access to websites unsuitable for children.

STILL MORE JOBS EXIST

The list of jobs that involve children in some way is extremely long. One way to find additional careers that involve working with children is to think of all the places in which children congregate and determine what jobs are associated with these gatherings. For example, in December children stand patiently in line to visit Santa Claus. Thus, holiday part-time jobs exist for would-be Santa Clauses and their helpers. Children also are frequently seen in restaurants that combine food service with an opportunity to play games. Jobs are available in these restaurants, both as staff and game supervisors.

Some jobs associated with children serve children living in other countries. Nightly newscasts often show the plight of children living in third world countries who are impoverished and living without adequate food, clothing, education, shelter, or health care. UNICEF (United Nations Children's Fund) is one organization involved in helping these children. Jobs at organizations like UNICEF are difficult to get because so many highly qualified people apply for them. For example, at UNICEF, minimum employment requirements include a university degree and postgraduate study in a development-related discipline such as nutrition, primary education, public health, or social welfare. Several years of professional work in a developing country is also required, as is written and spoken fluency in English and French, Spanish, or Arabic.

Two programs of the federal government, the Peace Corps and AmeriCorps, provide opportunities to help children. Peace Corps volunteers are sent around the world to help young children learn English and to teach good nutrition to mothers. AmeriCorps is a new national service initiative in which members receive a stipend along with many educational opportunities in exchange for their service. AmeriCorps offers the opportunity to work directly with children in child care centers as well as at CCR&R agencies, where they work with children, parents, and child care providers.

In addition, many jobs in science have benefitted and continue to benefit children. Jonas Salk made the first polio vaccine, which has nearly eradicated this disease in the United States. Other researchers in laboratories across the country are working diligently to conquer serious childhood diseases such as cancer, muscular dystrophy, and Tay-Sachs disease. Any person could become an instant hero upon conquering one of these diseases.

By browsing through newspaper ads and career handbooks, it is possible to continually discover new careers involving working with children. No matter what career choice individuals make, they will gain immense satisfaction from working with children.

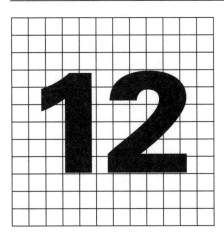

FINDING A JOB WORKING WITH CHILDREN

Hillary Rodham Clinton has said frequently that it takes a village to raise a child. In today's world, this is exactly what is happening as more people than ever before have careers involving the care of children. This book has explored careers that let people be involved in some way in children's lives. Some of these careers can have a dramatic impact on the life of the child—the skilled surgeon who repairs a defective heart valve, the teacher who inspires a learning-disabled child to try for a college scholarship, the foster parent who buoys a child's self-esteem. Other careers only affect a child's life for a brief period of time—a clown who makes a child laugh or a coach who comforts a child who strikes out in baseball. This final chapter looks at the prospects of finding a job that involves the care and well-being of children and describes the best way of finding and getting one of these jobs.

WHERE THE JOBS ARE

The greatest numbers of jobs for those seeking careers that involve children are in two areas: child care and teaching. The demand for child care workers—whether they are caring for children in their own homes, in child care centers, or in the children's homes—is steadily increasing due to two factors: in the majority of homes both parents work and the turnover rate for employees in this area is very high. With school enrollment up and class size declining, the demand for teachers is expected to grow about as fast as the average for all occupations through 2006.

The employment of social workers, health care workers, police officers in juvenile bureaus, sports instructors, and recreation specialists will grow at about the same rate as all other occupations. Many of the new jobs in these areas will come from the replacement of current workers who retire or find another job. Individuals looking for jobs as juvenile judges or within most segments of the entertainment field face keen competition.

FINDING A JOB

The perfect job search is the one that results in being hired for the desired job in a minimal amount of time. The right place to look for a job does depend to a certain extent on the type of job. Juvenile judges do not find jobs by searching the want ads, but child care workers can and do find jobs by pursuing these pages. Teachers, social workers, and health care professionals also can get job leads through newspaper ads.

Traditionally, the newspaper has been a good starting point for investigating the job market. Now, many people begin their job search on the Internet, where they can find an incredible number of employment opportunities with just a few clicks of a mouse. Beyond sites that list thousands of openings for a wide variety of careers, there are sites for professional organizations, college placement bureaus, private companies, and federal, state, and local government units. It is also possible to use the Internet to find out average salaries for careers in different parts of the United States. For many jobs, it is even possible to apply on-line.

Employment agencies can be effective sources of jobs for certain child care careers. Some agencies actually specialize in finding jobs for teachers, nannies, baby-sitters, and some health care positions. By visiting one of these agencies, job seekers can obtain a quick overview of the types of jobs available in a community.

College graduates should always investigate the services of their school's placement bureau. These bureaus usually serve not only recent graduates but all alumni. Placement bureaus will have long lists of job openings with fairly detailed information about each job. Teachers, social workers, and health care professionals can often find jobs by using this resource. Furthermore, placement bureaus often offer information and workshops on getting a job, from how to write a résumé to handling the job interview.

Social workers typically work for public or private agencies, while teachers will work for a school district. A good way to find jobs for these professions is by making direct contact with the organization where the job seeker wants to work. A phone call or a letter will swiftly provide information about employment opportunities and how to apply for jobs.

Job seekers need to talk about their search. Someone may know a third-grade teacher who is moving across the country, a police department that has the money to hire several new officers in the juvenile bureau, or a private adoption agency that is looking for a part-time social worker. Besides talking to friends and relatives, it is helpful to network with those who are employed in the areas where job seekers want work. These people often know where job openings are and about positions that may be available in the near future.

WRITING THE RÉSUMÉ

Almost every job seeker needs a résumé that details his or her work experience and educational background. Child care centers want to know the background of each potential employee, as do schools, child welfare agencies, and police departments. Parents want to know if baby-sitters and nannies who will be caring for their children have references available. When employers hire people to work with children, they need to be sure they are employing well-qualified individuals.

The résumé serves as an individual's introduction to an employer. It is a very important document that can lead to employment interviews. Résumés must clearly present an individual's qualifications to be effective. Shelves of books in bookstores purport to tell how to write a winning résumé. College placement bureaus, employment agencies, and websites will also have information on how to create résumés that get people hired. Before creating a résumé, job seekers should study sample résumés, especially those of individuals who are employed in the area in which they are looking for a job.

Here are some basic hints for writing an effective résumé:

1. Résumés should not have extra-wide margins. A small, difficult-to-read type size should not be used just to fit more information on the résumé.

2. Most résumés should be one page in length. First-time job seekers should not go beyond this limit. More experienced workers should not have more than two pages unless they would be excluding vital education or work experiences.

3. Résumés must be proofread carefully for spelling and grammatical errors. Computer spell-check programs can help in this task. Always have someone check the résumé for errors that may have been overlooked by a computer program or yourself.

4. A heading, work experience section, and education section should always be included on a résumé. If a specific position is sought, the résumé writer should state this in a job objective. Licenses and certificates and professional memberships should only be listed if they pertain to the job that is being sought. Special skills, especially computer skills and knowledge of foreign languages, should be included in résumés. A section should also be used for honors if the honors are of significant distinction. References should not be given on the résumé, but their availability should be stated.

5. A résumé should always be accompanied by a typed cover letter.

The following résumés are actual résumés of job seekers looking for positions (recreation worker, nanny, child care center director, psychologist, and teacher) that involve the care of children.

Timothy N. Davis

465 Clark Drive
Eau Claire, WI 54703
(715) 555-8927

Objective:	To work with children in a recreational setting.
Education:	University of Minnesota, 1996–2000 B.S. in Parks and Recreation

Experience:

6/00–9/00	**Eau Claire Parks Department**, Eau Claire, WI Recreation Worker Organized sports teams and leagues for children under 10. Created programs for each week's sports activities. Taught the correct use of facilities and equipment.
6/99–8/99	**Wisconsin Wilderness Camp**, Three Lakes, WI Senior Camp Counselor Provided instruction in boating, swimming, and canoeing. Lead three-day canoe trips each session. Supervised eight counselors and planned all camp water activities.
6/98–8/98	Camp Counselor Responsible for daily living and general socialization of 10 boys. Set up camp physical fitness program.

Capabilities:	Excellent organizational skills Responsible Able to work well with young people Skilled in working independently
Achievements:	Boy Scouts of America, Eagle Scout, 1996 Certified in Water Safety and CPR
References:	Available upon request.

Georgia Lowell
46 Red Oak Drive
Greenwood, IN 46142
(317) 555-6242

OBJECTIVE: To provide loving care for children in a safe, creative environment.

EDUCATION: Vincennes University, Vincennes, IN
Child Care Professional Nanny Certification, Fall 2000

Theory course work: Infant-Toddler and Early Childhood Care
Nutrition for Child Care Administration and Educators
Marriage and Family Psychology of Growth and Change
The Nanny as a Professional
Home Management and Family Communications

EXPERIENCE:

10/99–Present   *Field Placement*
Vincennes, IN

Work 20 hours a week for a sponsorship family. Provide loving care for a $4\frac{1}{2}$-year-old and a 6-month-old. Duties include supplying basic infant care and stimulation, planning and engaging in age-appropriate activities with preschooler, and performing light housekeeping duties.

9/98–8/99   *Assistant Teacher*, Greenwood Community Preschool
Greenwood, IN

Taught a classroom of children aged $2\frac{1}{2}$ to $3\frac{1}{2}$ years. Responsibilities included providing instruction in age-appropriate activities, implementing daily schedule, assisting children with developmental skills to prepare them for transition to 3-to-6-year-old classrooms, and holding parent-teacher conferences.

6/97–8/99   *Teacher Aide*, Greenwood Community Preschool
Greenwood, IN

Duties included opening the school, teaching in the "practical life" learning center area, watching children who took naps, leading group singing sessions, and performing general housekeeping tasks.

REFERENCES: Available upon request.

Mary N. Young
350 Kelton Avenue • Los Angeles, CA 90024 • (310) 555-1501

Experience:

Center Director

Sunshine Center, Los Angeles, CA
Center Capacity: 112 preschool children, 20 infants, 56 kindergartners, 35 staff

Maintain optimum enrollment by projecting openings and filling vacancies. Coordinate children's classrooms by age groupings. Foster open relationship with parents and children. Interview, support, evaluate, counsel, and dismiss staff as necessary. Ensure center compliance with state regulations. Assign staff schedule to ensure proper coverage. Maintain staff and children's records. Administer basic first aid and medications as necessary. Write and publish monthly parent and staff newsletter. (8/97–Present)

Center Director

YMCA, Los Angeles, CA

Supervised staff and provided written performance evaluations. Established emergency procedures. Maintained records of children and staff. Responsible for the arrangement, appearance, decor, and learning environment on site. Led staff and Parent Advisory Committee meetings. Turned in monthly reports including cash advance forms and receipts, staff salary projections, staff time sheets, and payroll information. (6/96–8/97)

Teacher

Department of Education, Woodbrook Elementary, San Jose, CA

Serviced children with low or no English proficiency with varied whole-language approach. Hands-on sensorial experiences were required to expose children to American culture as well as language. Monitored children once English proficiency was established to ensure academic success. (8/95–6/96)

Teacher

Skiles Test Elementary School, San Francisco, CA

Planned and implemented lessons to guide children in development in the following areas: social independence, problem solving, gross and fine motor development, language, music, art, reading, math readiness, and exposure to science. Provided in-depth written evaluations on each child's development in each of these categories quarterly. Met with parents to discuss concerns and achievements biannually in formal conferences. (8/92–6/95)

Education:

University of San Francisco, San Francisco, CA
B.A., Education, 1992

References:

Upon request.

Sharon P. Johnson
1016 Willow Lane
New Haven, OH 57220
(513) 555-2537

POSITION DESIRED: School Psychologist

PERSONAL: Speak fluent Spanish. Proficient in Word, PowerPoint, and Excel.

EDUCATION: North Salem University—B.A., Psychology (1997)

Bellaire University—M.A., Psychology (1998)

Williamshire University—Ed.S., School Psychology (2000)

CERTIFICATION: School Psychologist I

WORK EXPERIENCE:

9/99–8/00   **Williamshire University Counseling and Testing Clinic/Department**
Position: Graduate Assistant (20 hours/week)
Provided career counseling for college students.

6/99–8/99   **Kramer Clinic**
Position: Addictions Counselor
Counseled teenagers in group sessions in a residential clinic.

6/97–6/99   **Children's Services**
Position: Counselor
Worked with children in foster care.

OFFICES HELD/
MEMBERSHIPS: Williamshire University Graduate Council, Student Representative

Associate of Graduate Counselors at Williamshire University, Vice President

National Association of School Psychologists, Member

American Psychological Association, Member

REFERENCES: Furnished upon request.

Dana Alexander
32 Starmont Drive
Kalamazoo, MI 49002
(616) 555-6812

CAREER OBJECTIVE

A teaching position in an elementary school classroom for the mildly mentally handicapped.

EDUCATION

Bachelor of Science, December 1999
Major: Elementary Education
Endorsement: Special Education (MIMH)
Ball State University, Muncie, Indiana

Grades: 3.302/4.0 (major), 3.85/4.0 (endorsement), 3.49/4.0 (overall)

Honors: Kappa Delta Pi (Honor Society in Education)
3/98–present, Dean's List (5 times), EXEL Program

PROFESSIONAL EXPERIENCE

1/99–4/99   Student Teacher, Longfellow Elementary School, Muncie, Indiana.
Taught spelling, reading, math, handwriting, social studies, and language arts lessons in a first-grade classroom with 16 students.

WORK EXPERIENCE

6/99–8/99   Secretary, Kelly Services, Indianapolis, Indiana. Worked at Kraft Foodservice using Word and performed secretarial duties.

4/99–5/99   Substitute Teacher, Muncie Community Schools, Muncie, Indiana.
Taught grades one through six in all subject areas to handicapped.

8/96–12/98   Math Grader and Computer Lab Assistant, Ball State University,
Muncie, Indiana. Graded math exams, loaded computers, and helped students having problems with educational software.

ACTIVITIES

Volunteered to help an autistic child using the Sun-Rise program, 1/97–5/97.

REFERENCES
Available upon request.

WRITING THE COVER LETTER

The purpose of the cover letter is to introduce the job applicant, explain why the résumé has been sent, and request an interview. The following information should usually be included in the cover letter:

1. The writer's name and address, unless a personal letterhead is used

2. The date

3. The name and title of the person to whom the résumé is being sent and the organization name and address

4. The salutation: "Dear Mr. Jones," "Ms. Smith," "Dr. Johnson," or "To Whom It May Concern"

5. An opening paragraph explaining why the applicant is writing and stating the position being sought

6. One or more paragraphs pointing out why the applicant would like to work for the organization and the qualifications the applicant has

7. A final paragraph requesting an interview

8. The closing: "Sincerely," or "Yours truly," followed by the applicant's signature and name typed under the signature

Cover letters should not be more than one page in length. The tone of the letter should be formal and businesslike. The cover letters on the next pages were written by first-time job seekers.

MARGARET JONES
368 BIRCH DRIVE
KENOSHA, WI 53143
(414) 555-5604

April 17, 20__

Mr. Clark Adams, Principal
Clay Elementary School
3500 Main Street
Naperville, IL 60565

Dear Mr. Adams:

I will be graduating from the University of Wisconsin in May. I am seeking an elementary school teaching position in second grade.

My education from the University of Wisconsin has exposed me to the latest developments in the teaching profession. It has also given me the opportunity to participate in different classroom situations. I plan to continue my professional growth in the future by pursuing a master's degree in education.

Enclosed, you will find my résumé. A complete credentials file is available upon request through the University of Wisconsin: Educational Placement Office, 4600 Sunset Avenue, Madison, Wisconsin 53709, (608) 555-3000.

I would like to request an interview with the Clay School Corporation at this time. I may be contacted at the above address or phone number. Could you please send me informational literature on your school corporation? Thank you.

Sincerely,

Margaret Jones

Margaret Jones

Enclosure

MARK G. YOUNG

26430 HUDSON LANE
DOVER, DE 19901
(302) 555-8947

June 12, 20__

Mr. Peter Wiggins, Executive Director
Dover Department of Social Services
965 Park Avenue
Dover, DE 19901

Dear Mr. Wiggins:

     I am writing to inquire whether the Dover Department of Social Services has an opening for a social worker in your Children's Protective Services program. Having a bachelor's degree in social work and experience working with children at a women's shelter for the past two summers, I feel that I am well qualified to be a social worker.

     My volunteer experience as a Big Brother has taught me how to relate effectively with abused children. In addition, my 400 hours of supervised field experience has been in a Children's Protective Services program. This has acquainted me with the services abused children need.

     I would appreciate the opportunity to discuss my qualifications and abilities with you at length in an interview.

Sincerely,

Mark G. Young

Mark G. Young

Janet Lynn Gomez
3800 Alvarado Boulevard
San Antonio, TX 78243
(210) 555-4335

May 9, 20__

Dr. Colleen LeRoy
Children's Dental Clinic
5420 Ramona Avenue
Austin, TX 78501

Dear Dr. LeRoy:

I am writing in response to your advertisement in the Sunday edition of the *Austin American-Statesman* for a dental hygienist. The position greatly interests me, as I am especially interested in working with children.

I have just received my Texas dental hygienist license and am eager to begin my career. Furthermore, I have completed two years of college at Concordia University.

A résumé is enclosed that reflects my academic and work experience. I am confident that my background would make me an asset to the clinic.

I look forward to hearing from you soon. Thank you for your consideration.

Sincerely,

Janet Lynn Gomez

Janet Lynn Gomez

Enclosure

340 Bristol Drive
Richmond, VA 23285
(804) 555-8756
gstanton@aol.com

March 10, 20__

Harvey Gifford
Valley Tennis Club
20009 First Street NW
Santa Clara, CA 95054

Dear Mr. Gifford:

Roger Adams of the United States Tennis Association referred me to you because of your club's need for a professional to establish a junior program. I would be very interested in discussing this position with you.

I will be graduating from the University of San Francisco in May 20__ with a major in recreation. Besides working for the past two summers with the junior tennis program of the Santa Clara County Parks Department, I was a ranked junior player in California and a member of my college tennis team.

My résumé is enclosed for your review. I will call you on Friday to set up an appointment to talk about how I might be useful in setting up Valley Tennis Club's new youth program. I look forward to meeting with you.

Sincerely,

George Stanton

George Stanton

Enclosure

PREPARING FOR THE INTERVIEW

Job applicants need to think of interviews as information-sharing sessions. In preparing for an interview, they must determine how they want to describe themselves to the interviewer. At the same time, they need to consider what questions they have for the interviewer about the organization, because in every interview, the interviewer eventually asks, "Do you have any questions?"

Job applicants should never go into an interview unprepared. They need to be as diligent in their preparation as the president is before a press conference. The best preparation for prospective interviewees is to actually say aloud several times exactly what they would like the interviewer to know about themselves. They should also prepare answers to the following questions, which are frequently asked at interviews.

1. Why should this organization hire you?

2. What are your greatest strengths and weaknesses?

3. In what ways do you think you will make a contribution to this organization?

4. Why did you choose this career?

5. What are your long-range career objectives?

6. What two or three accomplishments in your life have given you the greatest satisfaction? Why?

7. Why did you decide to apply for a job with this organization?

8. How would you describe yourself?

9. How do you plan to achieve your career goals?

10. What motivates you to put forth your greatest effort?

Some job seekers find it helpful to hold practice interview sessions in which friends or family members ask them possible interview questions. Practicing answers to questions ahead of time makes answering similar questions much easier at the time of the interview.

Before any interview, job seekers must always find out as much as they can about the organization they are interviewing with and what their job duties in the position would be. For example, an applicant for the position of school psychologist needs to know if his or her position will involve primarily testing or counseling or some combination of these two responsibilities. Information about large organizations can be obtained by reading about them or visiting their websites. Some organizations have newsletters, which give applicants an idea of the feel and the tone of the organization. However, the information that most child care workers need is more likely to come from individuals actually working at the organization or in the job for which the person is applying.

Once the applicant has solidly prepared what he or she would like to say at the interview, it is time to consider some practical details. An outfit for the interview should be carefully chosen. It should be in keeping with company standards for the position being sought. Also, the applicant should become familiar with the route to the interview site in order to arrive early.

THE ACTUAL INTERVIEW

At large organizations, the first interview may be with a member of the human resources department to determine if the applicant is qualified. Subsequent interviews are likely to be with the staff member for whom the job seeker will be working. For example, a teacher applying for a job in a large school district is likely to interview with the human resources director first, and then, if this interview goes well, by the principal of the school where the teacher would be working. On the other hand, an applicant for a job at a small child care center will probably interview directly with the director of the center.

The first part of every interview is devoted to breaking the ice and establishing rapport. Even cliches about the weather may be exchanged. The heart of the interview occurs when applicants describe their qualifications in answer to questions from the interviewer. Interviewees should always listen very attentively to questions and should avoid negative comments and exaggerations. This is also the time to ask any questions the applicant has. These questions should be about work-related activities. It is inappropriate to ask about salaries and benefits until after a job has been offered. At the end of the interview, the job seeker should always express appreciation for the interview and ask for the job.

FOCUSING ON THE FUTURE

Once a job has been offered and accepted, job seekers who want to be involved with children are ready to start or continue careers that will bring them satisfaction. No matter what their careers are, they will receive smiles and hugs from little children and quiet or boisterous appreciation from older children. And it is not only the children who will applaud their work: the children's parents will, too. In fact, American society holds in great esteem those individuals who devote their lives to working with children.

APPENDIX: SOURCES OF ADDITIONAL INFORMATION

This section lists names and addresses of associations and other organizations that provide useful career information. By contacting these groups, individuals can find out about what specific careers are like, preparation for careers, typical salaries, job opportunities, and more.

CHAPTER 2: CHILD CARE CENTER CAREERS

Child Care Action Campaign (CCAC)
330 7th Avenue, 17th Floor
New York, NY 10001

Council for Early Childhood Professional Recognition (CECPR)
2460 16th Street NW
Washington, DC 20009
www.cdacouncil.org

National Association of Child Care Professionals
304-A Roanoke Street
Christiansburg, VA 24073

National Child Care Association (NCCA)
1029 Railroad Street NW
Conyers, GA 30207-5275
http://nccanct.org

National Coalition for Children's Centers
P.O. Box 258
Cascade, WI 53011

National School-Age Care Alliance (NSACA)
1137 Washington Street
Boston, MA 02124

CHAPTER 3: CHILD CARE CAREERS IN YOUR HOME

National Association for Family Child Care
525 5th Street SW, Suite A
Des Moines, IA 50309-4501
www.nafcc.org

National Association of Child Care Resource & Referral
   Agencies (NACCRRA)
1319 F Street NW, Suite 810
Washington, DC 20004
www.naccrra.org

CHAPTER 4: NANNY CAREER OPPORTUNITIES

American Council of Nanny Schools
Delta College
University Center, MI 48710
www.delta.edu

International Nanny Association (INA)
Station House, Suite 438
900 Haddon Avenue
Collingswood, NJ 08108
www.nanny.org

CHAPTER 5: BABY-SITTING CAREER OPPORTUNITIES

American Red Cross National Headquarters (ARC)
8111 Gatehouse Road
Falls Church, VA 22042

CHAPTER 6: EDUCATION CAREERS WORKING WITH CHILDREN

American Federation of Teachers
555 New Jersey Avenue NW
Washington, DC 20001

American Montessori Society
281 Park Avenue S., 6th Floor
New York, NY 10010

National Association for the Education of Young Children
(NAEYC)
1509 16th Street NW
Washington, DC 20036
www.naeyc.org

The National Education Association (NEA)
1201 16th Street NW
Washington, DC 20036-3290
www.nea.org

National Head Start Association
1651 Prince Street
Alexandria, VA 22314

CHAPTER 7: CHILDREN'S SPORTS AND RECREATION CAREERS

Sports

National Alliance for Youth Sports
2050 Vista Parkway
West Palm Beach, FL 33411-2718
www.nays.org

National Association for Girls and Women in Sport (NAGWS)
1900 Association Drive
Reston, VA 22091
www.aahperd.org

National Association for Sport and Physical Education
1900 Association Drive
Reston, VA 22091
www.aahperd.org

National Council of Athletic Training
1900 Association Drive
Reston, VA 22091
www.aahperd.org

Recreation

The American Alliance for Health, Physical Education,
  Recreation and Dance (AAHPERD)

1900 Association Drive
Reston, VA 22091
www.aahperd.org

The American Association for Leisure and Recreation
   (AALR)
1900 Association Drive
Reston, VA 22091

American Camping Association
Bradford Woods
5000 State Road 67 North
Martinsville, IN 46151-7902

National Employee Services and Recreation Association
2211 York Road, Suite 207
Oak Brook, IL 60521-2371

National Recreation and Park Association
2775 South Quincy Street, Suite 300
Arlington, VA 22206
www.nrpa.org

YMCA of the USA
101 North Wacker Drive
Chicago, IL 60606

CHAPTER 8: CHILDREN'S HEALTH CAREERS

General

American Dental Association
211 East Chicago Avenue, Suite 1814
Chicago, IL 60611-2678
www.ada.org

American Dental Hygienists Association
444 North Michigan Avenue, Suite 3400
Chicago, IL 60611
www.adha.org

American Medical Association
515 North State Street
Chicago, IL 60610-4377
www.ama-assn.org

American Nurses Association
600 Maryland Avenue SW
Washington, DC 20024
www.nursingworld.org

Association of American Medical Colleges
Section for Student Services
2450 N Street NW
Washington, DC 20037-1131
www.aamc.org

National League for Nursing
350 Hudson Street
New York, NY 10014

Pediatric Medicine

American Academy of Pediatric Dentistry
211 East Chicago Avenue, Suite 700
Chicago, IL 60611-2616

American Academy of Pediatrics
141 Northwest Point Boulevard
P.O. Box 927
Elk Grove Village, IL 60009-0927
www.aap.org

American Pediatric Society
3400 Research Forest Drive, Suite B7
Spring, TX 77381

American Society of Dentistry for Children (ASDC)
875 North Michigan Avenue, Suite 4040
Chicago, IL 60611

Association for the Care of Children's Health (ACCH)
19 Mantau Road
Mount Royal, NJ 08061
www.acch.org

National Association of Children's Hospitals and Related
  Institutions
401 Wythe Street
Alexandria, VA 22314

National Association of Pediatric Nurse Associates and
  Practitioners (NAPNAP)

1101 Kings Highway N., Suite 206
Cherry Hill, NJ 08034-1931
www.napnap.org

Counseling
Troubled Children

American Academy of Child & Adolescent Psychiatry (AACAP)
3615 Wisconsin Avenue NW
Washington, DC 20016-3007
www.aacap.org

American Association of Children's Residential Centers
440 1st Street NW, Suite 310
Washington, DC 20001

American Association of Psychiatric Services for Children
220 Hibiscus Drive
Rochester, NY 14618

American Counseling Association
5999 Stevenson Avenue
Alexandria, VA 22304-3300

American Psychiatric Association (APA)
1400 K Street NW
Washington, DC 20005
www.psych.org

American Psychological Association
750 1st Street NE
Washington, DC 20002-4242
www.apa.org

Speech-Language
Pathology

American Speech-Language-Hearing Association
10801 Rockville Pike
Rockville, MD 20852
www.asha.org

CHAPTER 9: CAREERS ENSURING THE WELFARE OF CHILDREN

Social Workers

Association of Boys & Girls Club Professionals
c/o Boys & Girls Club of the Suncoast
5111 66th Street N., Suite 200
St. Petersburg, FL 33709

Big Brothers Big Sisters of America (BBBSA)
230 North 13th Street
Philadelphia, PA 19107

Child Welfare League of America (CWLA)
440 1st Street NW, Suite 310
Washington, DC 20001
www.cwla.org

Children's Defense Fund
25 East Street NW
Washington, DC 20001

Council on Social Work Education
1600 Duke Street
Alexandria, VA 22314-3421

National Association of School Psychologists
4030 East West Highway, Suite 402
Bethesda, MD 20814

National Association of Social Workers
750 1st Street NE, Suite 700
Washington, DC 20002-4241
www.naswdc.org

National Committee to Prevent Child Abuse
332 South Michigan Avenue, Suite 1600
Chicago, IL 60604-4357
www.childabuse.org

National Council on Child Abuse and Family Violence
1155 Connecticut Avenue NW, Suite 400
Washington, DC 20036

Police Officers

International Juvenile Officers Association
59 7th Street
Garden City Park, NY 11040

Juvenile Justice

American Bar Association, Young Lawyers Division
750 North Lake Shore Drive
Chicago, IL 60611-6281

American Judges Association
National Center for State Courts
300 Newport Avenue
Williamsburg, VA 23187-8798

Association of Child Advocates
1625 K Street NW, Suite 510
Washington, DC 20006

National Council of Juvenile and Family Court Judges
University of Nevada
P.O. Box 8970
Reno, NV 89507

National Court-Appointed Special Advocate
Association
100 West Harrison Street, No. 500
Seattle, WA 98119

CHAPTER 10: ARTS AND ENTERTAINMENT CAREERS WITH CHILDREN

Art Teachers

National Art Education Association
1916 Association Drive
Reston, VA 22091-1590

Children's Artists

Allied Artists of America
15 Gramercy Park South
New York, NY 10003

The American Institute of Graphic Arts
164 5th Avenue
New York, NY 10010

Society of Illustrators
128 East 63rd Street
New York, NY 10021

Music Teachers

Music Educators National Conference (MENC)
1806 Robert Fulton
Reston, VA 20190
www.menc.org

National Association of Schools of Music
11250 Roger Bacon Drive, Suite 21
Reston, VA 22091
www.arts-accredit.org

Dance Teachers

Dance Educators of America
Box 607
Pelham, NY 10803-0607

National Association of Schools of Dance (NASD)
11250 Roger Bacon Drive, Suite 21
Reston, VA 22091
www.arts-accredit.org

National Dance Association
1900 Association Drive
Reston, VA 20191

Professional Dance Teachers Association (PDTA)
P.O. Box 91
Waldwick, NJ 07463

Magicians

International Brotherhood of Magicians
11137 South Towne Square
St. Louis, MO 63123
www.magician.org

Clowns

Clowns of America, International
P.O. Box 6468
Lees Summit, MO 64064

**Children's Television
Shows**

Children's Film and Television Center
University of Southern California
School of Cinema/TV
850 West 34th Street
Los Angeles, CA 90089-2211

National Association of Broadcasters
1771 N Street NW
Washington, DC 20036

CHAPTER 11: MORE CAREERS WORKING WITH CHILDREN

Children's Librarians

American Library Association (ALA)
Office for Library Personnel Resources
50 East Huron Street
Chicago, IL 60611
www.ala.org

American Society for Information Science
8720 Georgia Avenue, Suite 501
Silver Spring, MD 20910
www.asis.org

Association for Library Service to Children
American Library Association
50 East Huron Street
Chicago, IL 60611
www.ala.org/alsc

Children's Photographers

Professional Photographers of America, Inc.
57 Forsyth Street, Suite 1600
Atlanta, GA 30303

Children's Museums

American Association of Museums
1575 I Street NW, Suite 400
Washington, DC 20005
www.aam-us.org

Association of Youth Museums
1775 K Street NW, Suite 595
Washington, DC 20006
www.aym.org

Society of American Archivists
527 South Wells, 5th Floor
Chicago, IL 60607
www.archivists.org

Religious Workers

The Jewish Theological Seminary of America (Conservative)
3080 Broadway
New York, NY 10027
www.jtsa.edu

National Council of Churches
Professional Church Leadership, Room 863
475 Riverside Drive
New York, NY 10115

The Rabbi Isaac Elchanan Theological Seminary (Orthodox)
2540 Amsterdam Avenue
New York, NY 10033

Rabbinical Placement Commission (Reform)
192 Lexington Avenue
New York, NY 10016

Children's Books

Children's Book Council
568 Broadway
New York, NY 10012

Children's Literature Association
P.O. Box 138
Battle Creek, MI 49016-0138

Society of Children's Book Writers & Illustrators
345 North Maple Drive, Suite 296
Beverly Hills, CA 90210
www.scbwi.org

**Children's Retail Store
Salespeople**

Childrenswear Manufacturers Association
Two Greentree Centre, Suite 225
Marlton, NJ 08053

**Creating Products
for Children**

National Retail Federation
327 7th Street NW, Suite 1000
Washington, DC 20004

Toy Manufacturers of America
1115 Broadway, Suite 400
New York, NY 10010

More Jobs

AmeriCorps
P.O. Box 340
Columbia, MD 21045
www.americorps.org

Peace Corps of the United States
1990 K Street NW
Washington, DC 20526
www.peacecorps.gov

United Nations Children's Fund (UNICEF)
3 United Nations Plaza
New York, NY 10017

CHAPTER 12: FINDING A JOB WORKING WITH CHILDREN

JOBTRAK.COM
www.jobtrak.com

The Riley Guide: Employment Opportunities and Job Resources
www.rileyguide.com

YAHOO! Careers
http://careers.yahoo.com